May God continue
to bless you.
  Joyce S. Thompson

Mildrey Whitelow
Madeline Barton
Beverly Barton
Ruby H Byrford
Mary H Akery
Theodora Howell

UNVEILING THE PAST

A History
of
Pleasant Green Missionary Baptist Church

Volume Two | 2003-2013

Loyce Stewart Thompson
and
The Pleasant Green Baptist Church History Committee

UNVEILING THE PAST
A History
of
Pleasant Green Missionary Baptist Church

Volume Two | 2003-2013

Loyce Stewart Thompson
and
The Pleasant Green Baptist Church History Committee

LOWBAR
PUBLISHING COMPANY

905 South Douglas Avenue • Nashville, Tennessee 37204
Phone: 615-972-2842
E-mail: Lowbarpublishingcompany@gmail.com
Web site: www.Lowbarbookstore.com

Printed in the United States of America, November 2014
LOWBAR PUBLISHING COMPANY
ISBN: 978-0-9862771-2-2
Nashville, Tennessee 37204
615-972-2842
E-mail: Lowbarpublishingcompany@gmail.com
Web site: www.Lowbarbookstore.com

For additional information, workshop, and seminars, here is how you may contact the church's historian:
Loyce S. Thompson
Pleasant Green Baptist Church
1410 Jefferson Street
Nashville, Tennessee 37208
615-876-0229

Editor and Text Compilationist: Loyce S. Thompson
Manuscript Compilationist: Calvin C. Barlow, Jr.
Graphic Layout: Norah S. Branch
Photographers : Odell Moss, Roxie Johnson , and Kerry Majors

All rights reserved solely by the Pleasant Green Historial Committee. No part of this book may be reproduced in any form without the permission of the Pleasant Green Historical Committee or publisher. The views expressed in this book are not those of the publisher.
© 2014

The Table of Contents

The History Committee vi

Dedication vii

The Pastor's Pen viii

Acknowledgements ix

Introduction x

Chapter One	A New Beginning	1
Chapter Two	A Shepherd is Called	5
Chapter Three	A Period of Reorganization	25
Chapter Four	New Leadership and a New Church Goal	28
Chapter Five	A Unique Partnership	31
Chapter Six	A Change in Leadership	33
Chapter Seven	A Time for Rebuilding	36
Chapter Eight	The Dawning of a New Day	40
Chapter Nine	New Directions for the Church	55
Chapter Ten	A Period of Discernment	61
Chapter Eleven	A New Season at Pleasant Green	64

APPENDICES

    A. The Church Covenant 85

    B. Church Organizations 86

    C. Momentous Events 94

The History Committee
of
Pleasant Green Baptist Church

Loyce Thompson – Chairperson
Wanda Scott - Co-Chairperson
*Nannie P Fort – Chairman Emeritus
Beverly Barton
Madeline Barton
Henry Berry
Ruby Burford
Doris Dobbins
Lifran Fort
Theodora Howell
Walbrey Whitelow
*Deceased

Dedication

The History Committee of Pleasant Green Missionary Baptist Church dedicates this book to the memory of Mrs. Nannie Parker Fort, who served as our church historian for many years. Her expertise, foresight, and perseverance in the preservation of church historical documents and memorabilia over the years helped immensely in compiling this manuscript.

-and-

We also dedicate this book to our 10th pastor, Reverend Michael R. Lomax for requesting that this manuscript be written during his tenure as pastor. He had the wisdom and foresight to realize that history is ongoing, and that the written documentation of history is extremely important.

The Pastor's Pen

Thank God for 129 years of building the Kingdom of God! It is a privilege to pastor the people of Pleasant Green Missionary Baptist Church. Pastoring is a very serious responsibility which should never be taken for granted and I am grateful to God for the opportunity to be your servant-leader.

The Scripture that comes to mind in contemplating the years ahead is Philippians 2:2-4 – "…then make my joy complete by being like-minded, having the same love, being one in spirit and of one mind. Do nothing out of selfish ambition or vain conceit. Rather, in humility value others above yourselves, not looking to your own interests but each of you to the interests of the others." When this lifestyle is embraced, we will fulfill our church theme of "Greatness Through Godly Growth."

The Book that you hold in your hands is a culmination of many hours of diligent work in producing a quality document for future generations to glean from the rich experiences and events of Pleasant Green. Special thanks to the visionary standard bearer, Sister Loyce Thompson, along with the entire History Committee for your diligence in producing this excellent work.

Christopher Jackson, Pastor

Acknowledgements

It is with sincere gratitude and appreciation that we acknowledge the following persons and organizations for their assistance in the production of this historical document:

Reverend Dr. Christopher Jackson for being a visionary leader who embraced the concept of a 2nd church history book and lent support to the History Committee in its efforts to continue the documentation of the history of Pleasant Green.

Reverend Dr. Samella Junior-Spence- for providing a wealth of factual information about the church and its activities in the weekly church bulletins during the years 2003 -2013.

The History Committee of Pleasant Green for their faithfulness to the tasks needed to see the production of this book to completion. Specifically, they are to be commended for the chronological organization of key information, documents and pictures, oral interviews, internet research, and critiquing, editing, and polishing the prose that comprises this manuscript.

We also give special thanks and recognition to Dr. Janet Walsh, and Dr. Evelyn Fancher, President and President- Emeritus, respectively, of the African- American Church Historians Association. From reading and critiquing the manuscript to facilitating the generous monetary scholarship for publication, we extend profound thanks and gratitude. We also acknowledge with gratitude their leadership in the African American Church Historians Association and their commitment to the importance of developing and recording church history throughout the community.

Our heartfelt appreciation is also extended to Bishop Calvin C. Barlow, publisher/CEO of Lowbar Publishing Company, for his invaluable advice and technical assistance with the publication of this book. Special thanks and gratitude is also extended to the following financial donors of Pleasant Green who exhibited faith in this project through personal contributions.

Mrs. Rebecca Jennings	Ms. Beverly Barton
Dr. Eunice Grisby	Ms. Madeline Barton
Mr. and Mrs. Kenneth McKay	Deacon Walbrey Whitelow
Mrs. Mary Hamby	Deacon Henry Berry
Mrs. Carmelia Cammon-Tate	Deacon Julius Hill

Finally, we must acknowledge and give thanks to Our Lord and Savior, Jesus Christ—for without HIM nothing is possible. To God Be the Glory!

Loyce S. Thompson
Church Historian and History Committee Chair

Introduction

At the time of the publication of this historical record, Pleasant Green Missionary Baptist Church will have reached an important milestone – the celebration of the 129th Anniversary of the church. It is, therefore, quite appropriate that we pause once again to look at other milestones which comprise the rich history of this great church. Our first history book, *Unveiling the Past, A History of Pleasant Green*, reached back to the church's inception – 1885 and carried us to the year 2002. This volume provided an accurate picture of how church life was conducted in the past, while providing insight into the goals, aspirations, and accomplishments of the congregation from 1885 to 2002.

Our current volume of the church's history will reveal the significant events, goals, and accomplishments of Pleasant Green Baptist Church during the past ten years – 2003 to 2013. It will continue the story of Pleasant Green where volume one ended. This document is written to emphasize the importance of continuing the documentation of church history with the realization that history is on-going and doesn't stop in time with a particular year.

Volume Two of *Unveiling the Past, A History of Pleasant Green* will reveal the joys and triumphs of the congregation as well as the disappointments and subsequent challenges. It will reveal the perseverance and determination of the church to survive and worship the Lord with gladness. Throughout these years, the church has held on to the belief that better times are on the horizon, and with God's grace the church will be able to accomplish much and exemplify our current church theme: "Greatness Through Godly Growth".

Finally, the History Committee of Pleasant Green hopes that this volume will serve as a foundation and inspiration to other able historians of the future to continue the documentation of church history.

Loyce S. Thompson
Church Historian and History
Committee Chair

A NEW BEGINNING

Over 100 years ago a small group of worshippers left their home church, which is the present day Mt. Zion Baptist Church, and formed a new church which they would call Pleasant Green Baptist Church. The name was chosen by one of the worshippers who was pleased with the progress of the new church. Upon glancing out of a window, he saw beautiful green fields and pastures and decided to call the church Pleasant Green. The year was 1885. 118 years have passed; this history begins in the year 2003. The name of the church remains unchanged, and the church still stands on the lot that was purchased in 1886.

2003 was a year in which the citizens of Nashville experienced the crippling effects of the largest snow event since 2000. On Janurary16 seven inches of snow fell in a single storm. Traffic came to a standstill as local schools and businesses all decided to dismiss employees early creating an overload of traffic on Nashville streets. Drivers were on the roads well into the evening hours trying to get home.

2003 was a transitional period for Pleasant Green. After the departure of Reverend Donald Smith, who served as pastor-elect from 2001 – 2002, Pleasant Green found itself once again without a leader. The Deacon Ministry emerged as the major source of leadership for the church at this time. The Deacon Ministry urged members to notify them immediately in the event of any crisis that might arise. Deacon Washington Dobbins and Deacon Richard Friley provided emergency contact phone numbers for such occasions. The Deacon Ministry also stressed to the congregation that plans for any program or meeting to be held at Pleasant Green had to be submitted to the Board of Deacons for approval. Deacon Washington Dobbins, chairman of the Deacon Ministry at this time, issued a special invitation to the congregation to attend weekly Prayer services on Wednesday nights at 7:15PM. This was designated as a special prayer time for strength, wisdom and unity. This special invitation, which appeared in the Church Mirror weekly, was designated as a special prayer time for guidance, wisdom, strength, and unity.

Several members of the Deacon Ministry also served as Church School teachers on a weekly basis. Those deacons were: Deacons Henry Stinson, Ross Fleming, Anne Cato. Brother Carlton Lewis also taught Church school classes for a month.

The Wednesday Night Bible Study teachers were Deacon Cordelia Wakefield, Dr. Frank Horton, and Sister Glynnis Johnson.

A Pulpit Supply Committee was formed which secured the services of local ministers to preach to the congregation on Sundays. Some of the ministers that were utilized at this time included: Dr. Forrest Harris, Reverend James Campbell, Reverend Janet Watson, Reverend James Shelton, Reverend Eugene Sewell, Reverend Dr. Frank Horton, Reverend Vincent Campbell, and Reverend Dr. Edith Kimbrough.

The Pleasant Green CDC (Community Development Corporation) was still active, and solicited contributions from the congregation through their employers.

The Trustee Ministry Chairperson, Sister Willa Hill, provided the congregation with the following update on repairs to the church:

1) Exterior painting
2) repaired upstairs windows
3) sealing the front entrance stairs
4) the installation of the new church marquee
5) installation of the new electronic key system

Additionally, Trustee Hill announced a Saturday Spring Cleaning Party to be held in April from 9:00 AM to 1:00 PM. The congregation was invited and a picnic lunch was provided. The tasks that were to be accomplished on this day included the following:

1) re-stripe the parking lot
2) spruce up the grounds
3) clean the church pew cushions

Church organizations continued to meet and have goals. Those organizations included:

1) **The Health Promotion Team,** led by Deacon Ann Cato, met on the 2nd Tuesdays of each month. They sponsored a Health Fair, which included health screenings, and also had an evening exercise class which met on Tuesdays from 6 -7PM in the church fellowship hall.

2) The Retirees Fellowship, led by Mrs. Mary Hamby, met on the 2nd and 4th Thursday of each month. Ms Beverly Barton taught Arts and Crafts at this time.

3) **The Layman League** met monthly under the leadership of Brother Isaac Roland.

Special events were few in number at this time. During the month of February, the church had its annual Black History Essay Contest. The essay topic this year was: "Black History: A People's Past Revisited." The church history book, *Unveiling the Past: History of Pleasant Green* was still available for purchase. The month also included a reception honoring Mrs. Betty Green, long time employee of the Matthew Walker Health Center, who was retiring and going back to Birmingham, Alabama to live.

A Pastor's Search Committee was formed in December 2002 for the purpose of filling the pulpit vacancy that was created by the departure of Reverend Donald Smith. The members of the committee were: Mrs. Beauty Stewart- Miller, Deacon Washington Dobbins, Ms. Willa Hill, Brother Carlton Lewis, Mrs. Evelyn Barbour, Mrs. Rose Hogg, and Mrs. Kay Kirkpatrick. The committee published a newsletter called "The Search" to keep the congregation informed about the pastoral search and progress. The chair of the search committee, Mrs. Beauty Stewart- Miller wrote the following letter to the congregation during the early stages of the search process:

Dear Sisters and Brothers in Christ:

The Search Committee is providing you with a summary of the things we have completed. The information is to keep you abreast of the work we are doing for you. This is an attempt to make this search a unified effort. We, the church body, must put forth a cohesive effort to choose the right person as a shepherd. When we ask you to participate through filling out survey forms, nomination forms, or any other form of involvement, this is done so that you can be a part of this process.

Pray for the Search Committee and the congregation. We ask God to instill in each of us patience. We will continue this search until we have a God-fearing shepherd "baptized in the Word. We cannot rush this process. We will receive a shepherd who has been touched by and led by God". Pray for insight and the ability to hear God and to follow His lead. May God smile upon each of you.

The Search Committee published the following **time line** for the search process:

December 8, 2002- Pastor's Profile survey to be in, extended to January 12, 2003.

December 16, 2002- Reports regarding how to secure a credit report, criminal background checklist, a list of places to advertise the position, and meeting dates submitted.

January 20, 2003- Survey forms reviewed, position announced. Meeting date changed to second and fourth Monday each month.

February 10, 2003- Mailed position announcement; included were: Vanderbilt Divinity School, American Baptist College, and United Seminary. Applications and instructions were mailed to persons with resumes on file.

March 31, 2003- Deadline for applications. A matrix has been developed to be used as we review resumes and applications. This matrix was compiled using information that YOU gave us on your survey.

POSITION ANNOUNCEMENT

Pleasant Green Missionary Baptist Church in Nashville, Tennessee is conducting a search to find a Pastor for the Pleasant Green Church Family. Pleasant Green Missionary Baptist Church is seeking a person of God who is honest, and is of sound spiritual and moral character. Desirable educational qualifications include a college and a degree from an accredited school of Theology. The applicant should have experience as a senior pastor of a church with an active membership of at least 300. Candidates should have progressive positions of responsibilities leading to successful leadership and management. These responsibilities should have occurred within the church with substantial leadership challenges and opportunities. Leadership in a Missionary Baptist Church is strongly desired. The candidate should give leadership to the spiritual affairs of the church, and participate in decision-making processes as well as public worship of "Good News" to the congregation. The successful candidate will work with existing church organizations and individuals at various levels as different needs arise in the church family. The successful candidate should possess strong interpersonal skills and be able to relate to persons of all ages.

Pleasant Green Missionary Baptist Church is located near downtown Nashville, in the midst of four prominent African-American universities. Nashville is a progressive, exciting city with excellent schools, hospitals, recreational facilities and communities. Pleasant Green offers a competitive salary that is commensurate with experience, skills, and academic preparation. Please forward resume and cover letter post-marked by March 31, 2003 to:

Pastor Search Committee
Mrs. Beauty Stewart-Miller, Chairperson
Pleasant Green Missionary Baptist Church
1410 Jefferson Street
Nashville, TN 37208

The Pastoral Search Committee administered a survey to the congregation of the church to determine the personal qualities that they wanted in the next pastor. The following "Character Profile" was formulated because of the survey.

CHARACTER PROFILE

PERSONAL

Married
Children
Family in same household
35 years of age (minimum)
Male/ Female

INTERPERSONAL SKILLS

Communicates effectively with all age groups
High morals
Trustworthy
Positive attitude
Committed
Honest
Has Integrity
Loyal
Diplomatic

EDUCATION

College/university degreed
Seminary degree
Accredited institutions

ABILITIES

Business management skills
Delegate responsibility
Visionary
Community oriented
Can make decisions for welfare of church
Good work ethics
Work history

MINISTERIAL SKILLS

Biblical Knowledge
Passionate and strong religious convictions
Biblically based
Effective communicator
Teacher
Sermons organized/related to today's world
Possesses a sense of humor
Teach the word, as well as live the word

A SHEPHERD IS CALLED

Pleasant Green held the election for pastor-elect on Sunday, November 9, 2003.

The electoral process that was used on this day was the secret ballot for members who were listed on the official church rolls. The winner of the election on this day was Reverend Dr. Alvin E. Miller, Sr.

Pleasant Green had thrived for over 100 years in part because of the strong leadership of its pastors. Two former pastors had unusually long terms of service. Reverend John Charles Fields served 36 years from 1901 – 1937, and Reverend Andrew l. Porter served 37 years, from 1944 -1982. Other pastors and interim pastors emerged as local leaders in the Nashville community. This list includes Dr. Forrest Harris, Sr., TNT (Tying Nashville Together) Founder and current president of American Baptist College; Reverend Inman Otey, realtor, entrepreneur, former TSU Career Development director; and the late Reverend Elizabeth K. Burgess, Language Arts Supervisor for Metropolitan Public Schools, and Administrative Assistant to the Director of Metropolitan Public Schools.

With this strong history of leadership, the Pleasant Green congregation was excited about the leadership potential of their Pastor-elect, Reverend Dr. Alvin E. Miller, Sr. Reverend Miller earned a Bachelor of Arts degree in Sociology from Eastern Kentucky, the Master of Divinity degree from Southern Baptist Theological Seminary, and the Doctor of Ministry degree from Oral Roberts University. Additionally, Dr. Miller came to Pleasant Green with a broad range of professional experience which included public school teacher, educational administrator, PFrison Chaplain, Drug-Free Community Coordinator, professional football player, and Military Pastor/ Chaplain. Not only had Reverend Miller excelled in academic, civic, and military pursuits, but he had also excelled in the area of sports.

Reverend Dr. Miller accepted the pastorate of Pleasant Green Baptist Church with great joy and humility. In the printed program for a church homecoming celebration, he said, "It is with great joy and humility that I have been placed here by the Master to continue His work at the church. The scriptural words found in Haggai 2:9 NIV speak to our vision: "The future glory of this Temple will be greater than its past glory, says the LORD Almighty. And in this place, I will bring peace. I, the Lord Almighty, have spoken!" With the guidance of God, the greatest Architect of the universe, the presence of the great Redeemer, Jesus Christ and the Holy Spirit, I see "The Best is Yet to Come.". The congregation of Pleasant Green also shared this vision and eagerly anticipated the future.

2004 was a year that began on a positive note with high expectations throughout the congregation. It had only been two months since the election of Reverend Dr. Alvin Miller, Sr. as Pastor-Elect of Pleasant Green. Reverend Miller was young – only 44 years old - energetic, and full of ideas for taking Pleasant Green to a higher level.

The highlight of the year was the installation service for Reverend Dr. Alvin Miller as the ninth pastor of Pleasant Green Baptist Church. Pre-Installation activities included a boat ride on the General Jackson at Opryland on Friday, April 17. An historic tour of Nashville for the pastor and his family followed on Saturday, August 28, 2004.

The installation service was held in the church sanctuary on Sunday, August 29, 2004 at 4:00 PM with Reverend Breonus Mitchell, Senior Pastor of Greater Grace Temple Church, as the guest speaker. Special music was provided by the Pleasant Green Sanctuary Choir, and the guest choirs from Greater Grace Temple and New Visions Baptist Church. Many local ministers, political figures, area college representatives and other community leaders were also participants on the program.

The Pastor's Installation service, at Pleasant Green, wasn't the only special event for 2004. Nationally, George W. Bush was re-elected President of the United States defeating Senator John Kerry. Nashville and the nation braced itself for four more years of a Republican administration.

Reverend Miller began his pastorate at Pleasant Green by making few changes.

His goal was to maintain peace, stability, and tranquility. Therefore, the order of worship service remained unchanged, the deacons had weekly leadership assignments for the worship service, and Bible study continued on Wednesday evenings at 6:00 PM. A subtle change was made in the music ministry with the addition of steel guitarist, Reverend Aubrey Ghent. Reverend Ghent accompanied the choir on selected songs, and played soulful, foot-tapping solos on his guitar.

Reverend Ghent's musical talents as a steel guitarist were noted in a national magazine. In the December 2004 issue of *Vintage Guitar*, there was a full- page article about Elder Aubrey Ghent under the heading: "Aubrey Ghent – Master of the Steel Guitar". The congregation of Pleasant Green was excited for Reverend Ghent having received this national honor, and prayed for God's continuous blessings on his musical journey toward higher heights.

A Christian Leadership Training Workshop was held for the entire congregation during Reverend Miller's first year as pastor. The Constitution and By-Laws Committee was also formed. The group consisted of seven members: two from the Deacon Board, and two from the Trustee Board. Ex-Officio members were: Pastor Miller; Chair of Deacons, Richard Friley; and Chair of Trustee, Carlton Lewis.

Pleasant Green continued to assist those who were less fortunate in the community through various community service projects. A can good drive began in October and continued through the 3rd Sunday in November. The goal was to feed 12 families. Three different schools identified three different families totaling nine families. The Pleasant Green congregation identified the remaining three families. A poinsettia sale was held in December to benefit the National Kidney Foundation of Tennessee.

In November 2004 several special events occurred at Pleasant Green including a Thanksgiving Fall Festival, which included Harvest Sunday. Harvest Sunday was a time when the entire congregation came to church dressed as they did in the olden days. Some of the ladies wore long dresses and bonnets; the men wore over-alls and plaid shirts, and the choir wore black with white Pilgrim collars. Additionally, there was a Joint Community Thanksgiving service held at the Ryman Auditorium in downtown Nashville involving area churches of all denominations. Reverend Miller was a guest speaker at this event.

A Solemn/Sacred Assembly was held on Friday, November 19 from 6:00PM until 12 midnight in the Church Sanctuary. The attire was casual / comfortable. Members were asked to read Joel 1: 13-20 for meditation and take no food or drink during that time period. Everyone met in the sanctuary for songs, prayers, a religious movie, discussion, pastoral teaching and more prayers and praising. The Ladies Aid Society held its 52nd Anniversary Celebration honoring Dr. Samella Junior-Spence and the late Trustee William Henry McGavock Johnson.

On Sunday, June 6 at 6:00 PM the church presented a concert featuring our own Reverend Aubrey V. Ghent, master steel guitarist along with Jerome Rhyant of Jerome Rhyant Ministries, Fort Pierce, Florida. The Pleasant Green Sanctuary Choir; Carl Dobbins, electric bass; Reverend Dr. Sherman Tribble, organist- pianist, and the Men's Chorus of Pleasant Green were also featured on the concert.

Several new deacons were in training at this time. They were Roxie Johnson, Tim Malone, Victoria Lynum, Bernard Sparks, and Lou McCain. The Ordination/Installation Service for these new deacons was held on Sunday, December 2, 2004 at 3:00PM in the church sanctuary.

Pleasant Green Missionary Baptist Church

INSTALLATION-INVESTITURE SERVICES

Ninth Pastor
Reverend Alvin Eugene Miller, Sr., D.Min.

10:00 A.M.   4:00 P.M.

Sunday, August 29, 2004
Pleasant Green Missionary Baptist Church
1410 Jefferson Street
Nashville, Tennessee 37204

THE INSTALLATION-INVESTITURE SERVICE
REVEREND DR. ALVIN E. MILLER, SR., D.MIN.
NINTH PASTOR
PLEASANT GREEN MISSIONARY BAPTIST CHURCH
4:00 P.M.
The Order of Service

The Service Prelude .... Selected Melodies
TheChoirs: "Hallelujah, Praise The LORD!" ("ACCLAMATION" from <u>GOSPEL MASS</u> R. Ray)
"In The Presence of Jehovah" (Geron Davis)
"The Glory of The LORD" (Gaither/Gaither)
Instrumentalists: Carl Dobbins, Bass; Elder Aubrey Ghent, Steel Guitar,
C. C. Johnson, Flute/Saxophone, George Woods, Tony Moorer, Trumpet
Reverend Dr. Sherman Roosevelt Tribble, Organ/Piano
Vocalist: Reverend Jerome Rhyant, Fort Pierce, Florida

The Seating of the Family
Marshal: Mrs. Wanda Scott
Mother: Mrs. Elizabeth Miller, West Palm Beach, Florida
Escort: Deacon Henry Stinson
Aunt: Mrs. Mary Alice Newton, West Palm Beach, Florida
Escort: Deacon Henry Berry
Sister: Ms Tamie Pennix, Washington, D. C.
Escort: Deacon Charles Gillespie
Brother and Sister-in-law: Reverend and Mrs. Charles Salem,III, St. Louis, MO
Daughter: Ms. Alvina Miller, Orlando, Florida
Escort: Brother Michael Lynum
Sons: Alvin Miller, Jr., Joshua Miller, Caleb Miller
Niece and Nephew: T'iara and Charles Salem, IV
The Seating of the Pastor
Reverend Dr. Alvin E. Miller, Sr.
Escort: Major Rufus Curry, Southern Command, United States Army

The Processional .... Clergy, Guests, Deacons, Trustees, Search Committee, Church Leaders
Marshals: Trustee Paul Miller and Brother Preston Mitchell
"We're Marching to Zion" (Watts-Lowry)
1. Come, we that love the Lord, and let our joys be known. Join in a song with sweet accord, and thus surround the throne. .
2. Let those refuse to sing who never knew our God; But children of the heav'nly King . . . may speak their joys abroad, . .
3. The hill of Zion yields a thousand sacred sweets before we reach the heav'nly fields . . .or walk the golden streets . . .
Chorus: We're marching to Zion, beautiful, beautiful Zion. We're marching upward to Zion, the beautiful city of GOD."
**

The Call to Worship .... Reverend William L. Barnes
Charter Member, Tying Nashville Together

Choirs:	*" Let everything that has breath praise the LORD! Praise the LORD!"*
Leader:	Praise waiteth for Thee, O GOD, in Zion, and unto THEE shall the vow be performed. O THOU that hearest prayer, unto THEE shall all flesh come.
People:	**Blessed is the man whom THOU chooses, and causes to approach unto THEE, That He may dwell in THY courts: we shall be satisfied with the goodness of THY house, even THY Holy Temple. "** (Psalm 65:1-2,4)
ALL:	**"How beautiful upon the mountains are the feet of those who bring good news, who proclaim peace, who bring good tidings, who proclaim salvation, who say to Zion, your GOD reigns."** (Isaiah 52:7)

The Anthem-Hymn . . . . Pleasant Green Sanctuary Choir
New Visions Baptist Church Voices of Visions Choir
"Lift Up Your Heads" (Ashford)
Soloist: Mrs. Sarah Wilhoite

The Congregation: "All hail the power of Jesus' Name; Let angels prostrate fall.
Bring forth the royal diadem and crown Him LORD of all . . . ."

The Invocation . . . . Reverend Raymond Bowman
Pastor, Spruce Street Baptist Church

The Introit . . . . Combined Choirs
" My Tribute" (Crouch)
Soloist: Mrs. Aggie Loyal

The Welcome . . . . Trustee Carlton Lewis
Chairman, Pleasant Green Missionary Baptist Church Board of Trustees

The Occasion . . . . Deacon Richard C. Friley
Chairman, Pleasant Green Missionary Baptist Church Board of Deacons

The Liturgical Dance . . . . Pleasant Green Baptist Church Youth Dancers
'Something About That Name" (Kirk Franklin)
Choreographer/Director: Ms. Elease Jones, Student, Fisk University
Youth Department: Sponsor: Mrs. Kay Kirkpatrick
Jessica Friley, Davida Majors, Michelle Lynum, Glynis Kirkpatrick, Marquisha Lawrence

The Greetings . . . . Reverend George T. Brooks, Sr.
Pastor, St. James Missionary Baptist Church
Director, Congress of Christian Works, National Baptist Convention of America, Inc.

Reverend Dr. William Buchanan
Pastor, Fifteenth Avenue Baptist Church
Dean , American Baptist College
Representative, Tennessee Baptist Missionary & Educational Convention

The Honorable Howard Gentry
Vice Mayor, Nashville-Davidson County, Nashville, Tennessee

Reverend Inman Otey
Minister, Zion New Jerusalem Church
Former Interim Pastor, Pleasant Green Missionary Baptist Church

Reverend V. H. Sonnye Dixon
Pastor, Hobson United Methodist Church
President, NAACP

Reverend Neal Darby, Jr.
Executive Director, Nashville Black Chamber of Commerce

The Music: ... "You'll Never Walk Alone" (Hammerstein-Rodgers) .... Women's Chorus
Soloist: Reverend Neal Darby, Jr.

Major Rufus Curry
Southern Command, United States Army

Mrs. Rosetta Miller Perry
Owner/Publisher: Tennessee Tribune, Contempora Magazine, Media

Ms. Michelle Marrs
Executive Director, Matthew Walker Comprehensive Health Center

Dr. Phyllis F. Junior
Fisk University Faculty Representative, Board of Trustees

The Music .... Combined Choirs
"Marvelous" (Walter Hawkins)
Soloist: Trustee Angela Dobbins
Guest Director: Mrs. Sheila J. Calloway, New Visions Baptist Church
The Offertory .... Deacon Cordelia Wakefield
The Offertory Music .... "I Love to Praise HIM" .... Pleasant Green Men's Chorus
Soloist: Deacon Harry Barnett
The Offertory Prayer .... Deacon Walbrey W. Lawrence
*The Doxology
The Music .... Combined Choirs
"Order My Steps" (Burleigh)
Soloist: Louis King, Jr.
Guest Director: Mrs. Avis Junior Woodard, New Visions Baptist Church
The Scriptures
    The Old Testament: *Isaiah 61:1-6* .... Dr. Charles E. McGowan
President, The Operation Andrew Group
    The Old Testament: *Psalm 1* .... Reverend Charles Salem, III, Brother
    The New Testament: Gospel: *John 10:1-16* .... Reverend C. C. Barlow, Jr.
Moderator, Stones River District Association
    The New Testament: Epistle: *1 Peter 5:1-11* .... Reverend Victor L. Michael Singletary
Pastor, First Baptist Church, Capitol Hill
*The Gloria Patri
The Introduction of the Speaker .... Reverend Dr. Sherman R. Tribble
Pastor, New Visions Baptist Church

The Music. ... . Greater Grace Temple Choir

The Sermon .... Reverend Breonus M. Mitchell
Founder and Senior Pastor, Greater Grace Temple Church
The Invitation to Discipleship .... Reverend Breonus M. Mitchell
*The Hymn-of-Invitation .... Greater Grace Temple Choir

The Music .... Choirs and Congregation
"Make us one, Lord; make us one. Holy Spirit, make us one.
Let Your love flow so the world will know we are one in You." (Cymbala)
The Installation .... Reverend James Thomas
Pastor, Jefferson Street Missionary Baptist Church

The Charge to the Pastor .... Reverend James Thomas
The Charge to the Congregation .... Reverend Enoch Fuzz
Pastor, Corinthian Baptist Church
President, Interdenominational Ministers' Fellowship
The Prayer of Installation .... Reverend Dr. Chestina Mitchell Archibald
Pastor, Key United Methodist Church, Murfreesboro
Director, Wesley Foundation, Fisk University
The Declaration and Hymn-of-Consecration .... Reverend James Thomas
"A charge to keep I have, A God to glorify, Who gave His Son my soul to save,
And fit it for the sky.
To serve the present age, my calling to fulfill, O may it all my power engage,
To do my Master's will." (Wesley-Mason)
The Investiture .... Reverend Dr. Marcel Kellar
Pastor, Antioch, Missionary Baptist Church

The Robe, Scarf and Hat: Deacons Richard Friley, John Lewis, Mrs. Elizabeth Miller(mother)
The Bible: Mrs. Evelyn Barbour(Search Committee), Reverend Charles Salem, III (brother)
The Keys: Trustee Carlton Lewis, DeSean Keyes (Youth), Alvin, Jr., Joshua & Caleb (Sons)

The Music .... Choirs and Congregation
"As you preach, preach the WORD; As you preach, preach the WORD.
Tell the world about JESUS, tell them about HIS love. Lift the Name of Jesus,
Tell all about HIS love. As you go, preach, the WORD, as you go, preach HIS WORD"
Soloist:: Reverend Jerome Rhyant, Fort Pierce, Florida
The Pastor's Response .... Reverend Dr. Alvin E. Miller, Sr.

The Closing Music .... Choirs and Congregation
"Total Praise" (Smallwood)
Liturgical Dancer: Mrs. Julia Moss
Youth Department Signers: Jessica Friley and Davida Majors
The Benediction .... Reverend Breonus M. Mitchell
The Recessional .... Reverend Dr. Sherman R. T
*The audience will please stand.

We welcome you and cordially invite you to the reception in the Pleasant Green Missionary Bapti
Church Fellowship Hall located on the lower level of the church.

Pictorial Highlights
of the
Installation – Investiture Services

For the
Ninth Pastor
Reverend Alvin Eugene Miller, Sr., D. Min

Pleasant Green and New Vision's Combined Choirs

The Male Chorus of Pleasant Green
Deacon Harry Barnett, Soloist

Reverend Breonus Mitchell, Guest Speaker
Founder and Senior Pastor of Greater Grace Temple

Trustee Carlton Lewis, and Youths Alvins Jr., Joshua, Caleb, and Desean

Mrs. Julia Moss performs a liturgical dance to "Total Praise."

Instrumentalists: Carl Dobbins, *Bass*; Elder Aubrey Ghent, *Steel Guitar*; George Woods, *Trumpet*; Dr. Sherman Tribble, *Organ and Piano*

Youth Liturgical Dancers

Mrs. Elizabeth Miller, Mother
Presents the hat to her son, Reverend Doctor Alvin Miller, Sr.

Deacon Richard Friley and Deacon John Lewis present the robe to Rev. Dr. Miller.

Mrs. Evelyn Barbour (Search Committee)
Presents the Bible to Bible to Rev. Dr. Miller.

Reverend James Thomas gives the charge to the Pastor Alvin Miller, Sr.

Reverend Doctor Alvin Miller, Sr. and Family

Congregation and Community gather for Installation Services.

Diaconate Ordination Service

Of

Leslie Drummond
Roxie Johnson
Victoria Lynum
Tim Malone
Bernard Sparks

Sunday, December 12, 2004
3:00PM
Pleasant Green Missionary Baptist Church
1410 Jefferson Street
Nashville, TN 37208

Reverend Dr. Alvin Miller, Sr., Pastor
Reverend Raymond Bowman, Speaker

The Program

The Prelude		
The Music	"Make Us One"	The Sanctuary Choir
The Seating of the Deacons		
The Seating of the Diaconal Candidates		
The Music	"I Love to Praise Him"	Deacon Harry Barnett, Soloist
The Call to Worship		Deacon Henry Berry
The Hymn	"Great is Thy Faithfulness"	The Sanctuary Choir
The Prayer		Reverend Dr. Edith Kimbrough
The Music	"God is Still Doing Great Things"	The Sanctuary Choir Trustee Angela Dobbins, Soloist
The Statement of Purpose		Deacon Richard Friley
The Solo	"Walk With Me"	Elder Aubrey Ghent
The Offertory		Deacon Cordelia Wakefield
Offertory Music	"I'm Gonna Live So God Can Use Me"	The Sanctuary Choir

Offertory Prayer	Deacon Cordelia Wakefield
The Scripture	Deacon Walbrey Whitelow-Lawrence
The Music .... "Center of my Joy"	Michaelangelo McCallister, Soloist
"Order My Steps"	Louis King, Jr., Soloist
The Presentation of the Speaker	Reverend Dr. Alvin E. Miller, Sr.
THE WORD of GOD	Reverend Raymond Bowman Pastor, Spruce Street Baptist Church
The Music .... "I Have Decided to Follow Jesus"	Choir and Congregation
The Presentation of the Diaconal Candidates	Reverend Dr. Alvin Miller, Sr.
The Ordination Charge	Reverend Dr. Alvin Miller, Sr.
The Ordination Prayer	Deacon Henry Stinson
The Laying On of Hands	Ministers and Deacons
The Hymn of Commitment .... " I Am Thine, O Lord"	Choir and Congregation

The Presentations:
- Certificates of Ordination
- The Deacon's Manual
- The Communion Kit

The Charge to the Church	Reverend Dr. Alvin E. Miller, Sr.
The Hymn .... "Stand Up For Jesus"	Choir and Congregation
The Remarks	Reverend Dr. Alvin E. Miller, Sr.
The Benediction	Reverend Raymond Bowman
The Right Hand of Fellowship	
The Reception	Fellowship Hall

Reverend Doctor Alvin Miller, Sr. Reads the Ordination Charge

Diaconal Candidates: (Seated) Victoria Lynum, Roxie Johnson, leslie Drummond

Deacon's Ministry - 2005
Pleasant Green Missionary Baptist Church

Front: Timothy (Tim) Malone, Dr. Leslie Drummond, Walbrey W. Lawrence, Henry Stinson, Dr. Ross Fleming, Jr., Roxie Johnson, Victoria D. Lynum, Richard C. Friley
Back: Bernard Sparks, Charles Gillespie, Harry Barnett, Henry (Hank) Berry, Washington Dobbins, Jr. (not pictured: William Johnson & Cordelia Wakefield)

A Period of Reorganization

New leadership often brings about new changes. Reverend Miller had just completed his first year as the newly installed pastor of Pleasant Green, and decided to make a few organizational changes in the church .Bible Study was expanded to include a mid-day session called "Munch with Miller". The time for this new Bible Study was from 11:30 AM to 12:45PM each Tuesday. The first thirty minutes was for prayers, fellowship, and discussion. 12:00 – 12:45 was the time that was designated for biblical teaching, praise and worship. Wednesday night Bible Study continued at 6:00 PM nightly.

Reverend Miller also sought to expand and improve the Sunday School. The time for Sunday morning worship changed from 10:00AM to 10:45AM to accommodate the newly expanded Sunday School. The new church schedule was:

    9:00 –9:15A.M. Light Refreshments
    9:15 – 10:30 A.M. Instructional Classes for all ages
    10:15 – 10:30 A.M. Assembly, Banner Awards in the Sanctuary
    10:45A.M. – Morning Worship begins

The new Sunday School Superintendent was Deacon Henry Berry, and the new Minister of Christian Education was Ms. Joyce Camp.

A New Birth Month Ministry also emerged at this time where the entire congregation was organized by birth months. Each birth month had a chairperson, and each birth month was asked to complete the following tasks:

    1) Raise or donate funds to help with the monthly church expenses
    2) Provide light refreshments for the Sunday School during the four
        Sundays of their month.
    3) Host a birthday party with a cake and other refreshments for the birth month honorees and congregation on the 4th Sunday. These birthday celebrations were held in the church fellowship hall immediately after morning worship.

A slight competition developed between the birth months to see which month could raise the most money. Most of the birth months gave checks to the church at the end of their month. The March Birth Month, chaired by Loyce Thompson, sold Commemorative Pleasant Green License Plates for $10.00 each. The license plates read:

    Pleasant Green Baptist Church
    Nashville, Tennessee
    Founded in 1885

While the Deacon Ministry and its duties and programs remained largely unchanged, Reverend Miller sought to re-organize the Trustee Ministry because of the expiration of some of the terms of the current trustees. On January 9, 2005, the membership was asked to nominate persons from the congregation to fill those vacancies on the Trustee Board. The deadline for submission of the names of nominees was January 31, 2005. By January 31, seventeen names had been turned in for consideration for the Trustee Ministry. Of the seventeen nominees, nine indicated that they would be willing to serve. They were Preston Mitchell, Harrison McCain, Joel Dobbins, Julia Moss, Henrietta McCallister, Isaac Burford, Loyce Thompson, and Bernardeen Fleming. Reverend Miller established regular office hours which were:

    Church Office Hours – Tuesday – Friday – 9:00 AM - @10:00PM

    Pastor's Office Hours – Tuesdays – 10:00AM – 5:00 PM

                    Wednesdays – 10:00 AM – 6:00 PM

After the departure of the church secretary, the church office hours remained intact through the assistance of the following persons:

    Monday- 9:00 -2:00 PM – Mary Hamby

    1:00 -3:00 PM – Elizabeth Hester

    Tuesday- 9:00 – 2:00PM – Lynn Shelton

    Wednesday- 10:00 -2:00PM – Sarah Wilhoite

    Thursday- 9:00 – 2:00PM – Lynn Shelton

    Friday – 11:00 – 2:00 PM – Rebecca Jennings

        10:00 – 2:00 PM – Joyce Camp

2005 was a year that was filled with many memorable events. Nationally, on January 20, George W. Bush was sworn in for a 2nd term as President of the United States. Locally, in Nashville, the Historic Joint Board Meeting of the Four National Baptist's Conventions met at Opryland Hotel in January. The four conventions were the Progressive National Baptist, USA; National Convention of America, Inc.; National Baptist USA, and the National Missionary Baptist Convention.

Pleasant Green was honored to have several dignitaries from the Progressive National Convention in attendance at the morning worship service on January 23. Our special guests on this day were Reverend Dr. Major Jemison, President of the Progressive National Convention, his cabinet, and other assisting laypersons. That afternoon Reverend Terry D. Streetor, pastor of Mt. Pleasant Baptist Church, Washington, D.C. delivered the message. The Pleasant Green Layman's League, Male Chorus, Sanctuary Choir, and Male ushers also assisted in the service.

In addition to regular morning worship services, the year was filled with several special church events. Those special events were:

    Health Committee plans Diabetes Day – July 16, 2005

    Omega Psi Phi Fraternity Revival – August 17-19

    Seniors Honors Saturday Brunch- July 23, 2005

    Financial Seminars to be Debt Free – Wednesdays, November 4 and November 11 @ 7:00 PM. Sister Roxie Johnson and Deborah Sparks were in charge. The seminars were centered on Dave Ramsey's Financial Peace Program.

Ordination Service for Dr. Samella Spence – Sunday, November 29 at 4:00 PM at New Visions Baptist Church.

The Layman League –hosted a three day Brotherhood Weekend Celebration in May. <u>On Friday</u>-Reverend Breonus Mitchell, Senior Pastor of Greater Grace Temple and his church were our guests. Dinner was served after the service.

<u>On Saturday</u>- a Prayer Breakfast was held at 9:00AM in the church fellowship hall with Reverend William R. Harris and the Male Chorus of Galilee Baptist Church as our guests.

<u>On Sunday</u> afternoon – a special concert featuring Male Choruses of several area churches was held in the main sanctuary.

January 2005 was also the month that our new pastor, Reverend Dr. Alvin Miller, had a book signing for his newly published book, *The Radical and Controversial Jesus*. The book signing was held in the church fellowship hall.

Pleasant Green extended a helping hand to others during 2005 through several community service projects. Those projects included:

TNT Bridges to Care Project, which involved sign-ups for health insurance and Doctor Assistance. In this program doctors have agreed to provide care based on a family's ability to pay.

Katrina Relief- members were asked to donate funds to help victims of the Hurricane Disaster in New Orleans, L.A. On Sunday, September 25, the church collected $1309.25 to be distributed to various organizations that were going to help the victims.

Thanksgiving baskets – Fifteen baskets were prepared and distributed to families of McKissack, Jones, and Buena Vista Schools. The delivery drivers were Bernard Sparks, Antoine Landers, and the Gillespie Family. Those preparing the baskets were Bernardeen Fleming, Florence Anderson, Herman "Hollie" Ford, Dolphus Spence, and Samella Spence.

2005 ended with the celebration of Reverend Miller's first anniversary. On December 18 Dr. Charles McGowan was the guest minister for the 11:00 worship service. A Green and White Festival Dinner was held immediately after the morning service. Presentations were made from each Deacon tribe, the Ladies Aid Society, and the Retirees Ministry.

NEW LEADERSHIP AND A NEW CHURCH GOAL

Change is sometimes greeted with mixed emotions. Some people feel that it is good, while some people feel that it is bad. Aristotle once said, Change in all things is sweet." Pearl Bailey said, "We must change in order to survive." Maya Angelou said, "If you don't like something change it; if you can't change it, change your attitude."

In 2006 the organization of the church continued to undergo changes. New leadership in the Sunday School emerged when Deacon Leslie Drummond became the new superintendent, and Sister Evelyn Barbour became the Assistant Superintendent. The newly elected Trustee Ministry continued their training sessions on the 2nd Tuesdays of each month. On March 5 Deacon Bernard Sparks was named as the new chairman of the Deacon Ministry. A new Membership Census Committee was also formed. Its purpose was to evaluate the membership status of each member and make adjustments in the membership roll of the church for accuracy.

The church roof debt was paid off and the kitchen underwent renovations. Mr. Mike Gilmore made new cabinet doors, added new sink fixtures, painted the kitchen, and added new lighting in the Fellowship Hall.

The Music Ministry expanded with the formation of a new gospel choir named The Voices of Praise. Initially, they were under the direction of Mr. Cedric Stevenson, and later Mrs. Mabel Little. They rehearsed on Wednesdays after Bible study, and later sang on the 4th Sundays during the morning services.

A newly formed Pastors Aid Ministry also emerged. The goals of this organization were to aid the pastor by supplying him with clean towels, handkerchiefs, fruit baskets, and juice baskets. They also helped to raise funds for the church by selling boxed home-cooked dinners on the First Sundays. Many in the congregation who ate out in restaurants regularly on Sundays now enjoyed home cooked meals at home.

One of the major goals of the church at this time was the purchase of a new state of the art bus/van. Several people in the church needed a ride to church each Sunday, and some of the members needed handicapped accessible transportation. This new van would accommodate the needs of both groups.

By Sunday, November 19, 2006, the church had raised **$20, 231.00** through individual pledges and donations. On the same day, Reverend Miller shared his plans with the congregation for raising the remaining $30,000.00. Plans were to have all monies on hand to pay cash for the bus within 12 months. Each ministry, organization, and deaconate tribe was asked to raise 1,000.00. The first three groups within the church to reach their goal would receive special recognition. The groups within the church that were asked for contributions were: Ministers Ministry, Diaconate tribes (14), Sunday School, Sanctuary Choir, Voices of Praise Choir, ladies Aid Society, Retirees, Usher Board, and the Layman League. The Birth Month Ministries were in place and had made previous donations to the church. For example, the January Birth Month Ministry donated $400.00 in February after they had raised funds.

The Sanctuary Choir raised the requested funds for the purchase of the bus by sponsoring a special evening worship service. Money was raised from the ads and patrons, and the collected offering from those attending the program. This special evening of worship was called the "Fine Arts Celebration". The service featured presentations in the areas of art, wood, sculpture, music, dance, drama, and poetry. The special guest artists in these areas were: Wilson Lee Jr., wood sculpture; Rev Sherman Tribble, organist; Benjamin Petty, rapper; Mrs. Ella Thompson, artist; Tony Moorer, trumpet soloist; C.C. Johnson, flutes/saxophone soloist; Michelle Lynum and Nandi Moss, dancers; Lifran Fort, artist; Briana Gillespie, artist; Caitlyn Gillespie, dancer; Brittany Gillespie, poet.

2006 was a year in which the church slogan, "The Best is Yet to Come", became a familiar phrase not only at Pleasant Green, but also throughout the city of Nashville, state of Tennessee and overseas. Reverend Miller's radio broadcasts of the Sunday service at Pleasant Green were now being heard locally on two radio stations – WNSG – 880 AM on Tuesdays at 9:30 and on WNGM – 1300 AM on Sundays at 7:30AM. Additionally, they were also heard in Memphis, TN on station WLRN 1380AM on Sundays at 10:30AM, and overseas in Nigeria.

Pastor Miller and the church received the following communication from Pastor Okorie Michael Ezeh in Nigeria:

P.O. Box 232 OJI-RIVER
EnuGU STATE Nigeria
February 10, 2006

Alvin Miller
The Best is Yet to Come
C70 wwer Nashville, TN 37218

Dear Beloved,
Greetings to you in Jesus Wonderful name. I am a local pastor of a small congregation here in the Interior village. I am writing to tell you that I have been listening to your broadcasts on Fridays on wwcr 15-825 mhz shortwave. It has been a source of inspiration and encouragement to me and I am praying for you daily.
Requests: 10 Please if you come across Life Application Study Bible (KLV) and Young's or Cruden's Complete Concordance send them to me. Used ones are acceptable. They will help me towards my Bible study and teachings as I have no money to attend a Bible College. 2) Please send me your messages on audio tapes. Your help will be received with an open mind.
I love to hearing from you soon. God bless you.

Your Brother in this service
Pastor Okorie Michael Ezeh

Pleasant Green did send Bibles to Pastor Ezeh in Nigeria.

Other special events during 2006 included the annual Black History Essay Contest. The topics for the essays were: "To Observe or Not to Observe Black History Month", and "Passages Remembered: A Future to Behold." The winners of the contest were: 1st place tie- DeSean Keyes and Delayna Keys and 2nd place tie Briana

Gillespie and Caitlyn Gillespie. Additionally, there was also the "Ques for Christ Revival": and a Christmas Cantata/ Drama featuring the Children's Choir called "Gather at the Manger," which was directed by Brother Herman Brady.

Pleasant Green was also involved in a special community service project with Meharry Medical College. Meharry and Pleasant Green sponsored a concert to benefit The Center for Women's Health. Grammy award winning artist Roberta Flack, and Yolanda Adams were the featured artists. The event was held at the Ryman Auditorium.

Later, in 2007 the ministerial staff of Pleasant Green expanded when Reverend Miller licensed three new ministers. Ministers Brenda Haywood and Pierre Moss preached their trial sermons on March 23. Minister Evelyn Barbour preached her trial sermon on August 12. All three received their licenses, an imprinted Bible, and the framed song, "Great is Thy Faithfulness." Minister Pierre Moss was later appointed to be the Minister of Children, Youth, and Young Adults. These newly licensed ministers joined the current staff of associate ministers, which included Reverends Veronica Dailey, Dana Forest, Edith Kimbrough, and Samella Junior-Spence.

The Usher Board also changed during this time period. They completed twelve weeks of training sessions conducted by Rev. Dr. Samella Junior-Spence. On Sunday, during morning worship service, they were awarded Certificates of Training and Merit May 27, 2007. The new president was Judy Sanders and the new members were: Kristen Brown, Marlinda Gillespie, Dannika Harris, Shirlyn Johnson, DeSean Keyes, Antoine Landers, Dominique Miller, Wanda Faye Solomon, Reginald Talley, and Tim Warfield. After their installation as new ushers, they would meet in the conference room each Sunday before service and discuss their role and duties in the church service. One of their recommendations was the addition of chairs and a bench in the hallway leading to the main sanctuary for people to sit in as needed.

Members of the Usher Board who had served previously for many years were also given certificates. They included: Jessie Baines, Harry Barnett, Mary Bateman, Louise Greer, Clarice Herrod, Richard Friley, Charles Gillespie, Willa Hill, Louis King, Sr., Richard Mayberry, Theo Phillips, Wanda Scott, Christine Bibbins, and Victoria Lynum.

There was a renewed focus on evangelism this year with the development of the "Go and Tell Ministry". The leader of this ministry was Reverend Dana Forest. The members of this evangelism team were: Deacons Henry Berry, Cordelia Wakefield, Leslie Drummond, Trustee Julia Moss, and Minister Evelyn Barbour. On Sunday afternoon, August 12, the "Go and Tell Ministry" held its consecration service. The members and audience received an inspired message from Elder H. Sawyers, and stirring songs from the West Harpeth Primitive Baptist Church Choir. Pastor Miller, assisted by Elder Sawyer and Reverend Dr. Samella Junior-Spence, anointed ministry personnel and prayed for their dedication, growth and zeal. They were admonished to go forth and tell; bring the lost to Christ. To keep this goal in the minds of the entire congregation, the following evangelism motto was repeated at the end of each morning worship service:

- ❖ Save a person, save a family
- ❖ Save a family, save a community
- ❖ Save a community, save a nation
- ❖ Save a nation, save the world

A Unique Partnership

The African-American church tradition has always included membership in various national church conventions, and church fellowships, or joint services with sister churches. These alliances between churches have proven to be very productive for all churches involved. In 2007 Pleasant Green Baptist Church embarked upon a unique partnership with The Church at Grace Park. This was truly a first for the members of Pleasant Green and also the city of Nashville. Pleasant Green was located in the heart of the inner city of Nashville with a congregation that was primarily African-American. The Church at Grace Park was located in White House, Tennessee with a congregation that was primarily Caucasian. When Reverend Miller announced the merger, he said. "It is an exciting opportunity for both churches and promises to take both churches and members on an adventurous and spiritual journey toward greater realms of service, relationships, and kingdom building."

The two churches formed this partnership with specific goals in mind. These goals were:

    1) to provide the churches multiple opportunities to worship and serve our God together.

    2) to join God on His mission together and demonstrate before a watching world the love of Jesus.

    3) to celebrate and model the "oneness" for which Jesus prayed the night before He was crucified

The two churches planned specific activities for the two groups to participate in together. Those activities included:.

    1) A Kindness Blitz on Jefferson Street – Sat, July 14 from 9:00 – 11;00 AM

    2) Friday Night at the Park – Friday August 10 from 6:30 – 9:30 PM

    Movie Fellowship – The movie *Second Chance* was shown.

    3) Pastor Miller's Anniversary- August 26 @ 4:00PM with Pastor Bob Cook, pastor of The Church at Grace Park, bringing the message

    4) Labor Day Picnic – Sunday, September 2 @ Grace Park

    5) Field Trip – Tour of Nashville – October 20

    6) Thanksgiving Supper @ Grace Park – Sunday November 2

    7) Christmas in the Park @ Grace Park Dec 14 – 15

    8) Watch Night Service/Kwanza Dinner and Celebration @ Pleasant Green December 31 8:00 PM

On Sunday, June 8, a picnic was held at Grace Park where approximately sixty-eight Pleasant Green members attended. The picnic concluded with the signing of the agreement of the partnership between the two churches.

Pleasant Green and the Church at Grace Park were chosen as Co-churches of the Week by the 700 Club on its world- wide television broadcast. The airings were on ABC at 9:00AM, and 11:00 AM on NBC (WSM Channel 4)

at 10:00AM. Both churches received plaques from the 700 Club. Pastor Miller and Pastor Cook did an excellent job of explaining the strategic partnership, philosophy, and the many joint activities of the two churches to bring about unity and increased kingdom building between the two communities.

Community Outreach was a dominant goal between Pleasant Green and the Church at Grace Park. The two churches, along with the Church at Fort Campbell, sponsored a Fisk University Benefit Concert that was held in the Fisk University Chapel. At this time Fisk University was experiencing a serious financial shortage. Fisk had been promised matching funds for any funds that were raised. Pleasant Green members, especially Fisk alumni, were asked to give at least $100.00 each. Blue and White envelopes were place in the pews for contributions. The 3rd Sundays in February and March were designated as donating days. On the day of the concert a check for $20,000 was presented to Fisk from the three churches.

Pleasant Green and The Church at Grace Park aligned themselves with the Bethel Church of the Nazarene, and Hosea Community Church for a Revival service. The Revival Service was held at Pleasant Green. Choirs from the four churches sang during the Revival service. Pleasant Green ushers and officers were asked to be available to host guests. Revival services continued on the following Monday evening at 7:00PM with Reverend Enoch Fuzz of Corinthian Baptist Church as the guest speaker.

Community outreach also extended to shared worship services with other churches. The Male Chorus of Pleasant Green sang at Mr. Calvary Baptist Church. The pastor and members of Hamilton Chapel attended our weekly Bible study, and Pleasant Green church officers, ushers, members, choir, and musicians worshipped at Elevated Baptist Church in Franklin, Kentucky for an afternoon service. Elevated Baptist Church and Reverend Lock were hosts extraordinaire providing a large spread of home-cooked foods. This was the beginning of a fellowship between the two churches. The congregation of Elevated Baptist Church traveled to Nashville later that year for a second afternoon worship service.

2007 was also a year in which Pleasant Green had a serious commitment on improving the health of its members. Dr. Randy Howard and Minister Brenda Haywood coordinated several health initiatives with this goal in mind. On April 13 a Health Fair was held at church with Dr. Keith Junior, Director of Physicians at United Neighborhood Health Center, as the facilitator. Twenty-three health and wellness experts shared a wealth of information. The event was well attended by approximately 100 people. Those who attended the event received health tips handouts, door prizes, and goodie bags. Pleasant Green was also involved in a city-wide health initiative called "World Tobacco Day". A service and celebration dinner was held for guests throughout the city. Pastor Miller served as host/ Master of Ceremonies for the event.

A Breast Cancer Forum was also held on October 13 @ 11:00 AM. Experts from Meharry Medical College and the Nashville Health Department provided demonstrations and discussion on breast- self-examinations, mammograms, and nutrition."Learning to Cook Healthy on a Budget" classes were offered at Bible study on the 1st Wednesdays of each month from 5:30 -7:30PM.

On Sunday afternoon, July 8, the Community and Health and Wellness Outreach Ministry, chaired by Minister Brenda Haywood, held its second "Unsung Heroes and Heroines Honors Celebration." Persons receiving this honor were: Deacon Harry Barnett, Mr. Lee Brown, Ms. Jackie Conwell, Mr. Joe David, Mr. Mike Gilmore, Mr. Maurice Haywood, Mrs. Elizabeth Hester, Dr. Keith Junior, Mr. Damon King. Trustee Louis King, Jr., Ms. Brenda Ivey Robinson, and Mr. J.T. Smith. All of the honorees received beautiful plaques and expressed deep appreciation for the recognition.

A CHANGE IN LEADERSHIP

Historically, 2008 was a banner year for African-Americans across the nation. Senator Barack Obama accepted the Democratic presidential nomination, becoming the first African-American to be elected by a major party as its nominee for the President of the United States on August 28. Later, on November 4th, Senator Barack Obama won the presidential election against Senator John McCain becoming the first African-American to be elected president of the United States. This was a time of great jubilation for African- Americans across the nation.

There were also changes in leadership at Pleasant Green at this time. On Sunday, May 18, 2008, Ordination Services were held for five ministers: Reverends Evelyn Barbour, Peggy Carney, Leslie Drummond, Brenda Haywood, and Pierre Moss. Reverend Greg Robinson preached a powerful ordination sermon. A reception, catered by Mrs. Marilyn Hiner, followed the service for the newly ordained ministers.

Sadly, on Father's Day, June 15, 2008, Reverend Miller tendered his resignation as Pastor of Pleasant Green to become effective on the fourth Sunday in July. The following written letter of resignation was later given to members of the congregation and the official Boards of Deacons and Trustees.

July 25, 2008

Dear Brothers and Sisters in CHRIST:

Guided by the Presence of the Holy Spirit, in the Name of JESUS CHRIST, and anchored in the Word of GOD, I in accord with my wife, write this letter to you.

On Sunday, June 15, 2008, near the end of our 10:45 A.M. worship service, I announced that the fourth Sunday in July (July 27, 2008) would be my last Sunday with you as your Pastor. I further anticipate that July 31, 2008 is the last day that I will be serving as your Pastor.

Over the past several years, I have had pastoral calls from many churches, but I felt none was a call from GOD for me to leave. Most recently, however, GOD has persisted in a call, and I must answer; I go where he leads me. I have struggled and wrestled through prayers, , thought, and deliberation, and I know I must answer the call to go. A little over a month ago, I did meet with some of the church officers and leaders at the close of Bible study to let them know about the possibility of answering GOD"s call to another church, and the struggle with which I was wrestling. It is now clear and I did make the announcement as stated above.

I give thanks to GOD and you for the five years I have served as Pastor here. I am reminded of the scriptural passages in 2 Corinthians 2: 17b: " *„in Christ, we speak before GOD with sincerity. Like men sent from GOD*", and Colossians 3: 17: " *And whatever you do, whether in word or deed, do it all in the Name of the LORD Through trials, triumphs and adversity, in times of tears, joys JESUS, giving thanks to GOD the father, through HIM.*", sorrows, prayers, and praise, I have served as your Pastor driven by GOD's word, guided by the Holy Spirit and acting in the Name of JESUS as together we have worked and grown in singleness of purpose to fulfill the mission of Kingdom building, soul saving and reaching others with our time, talents and resources. I sincerely thank you for your support, cooperation, and "maintaining the unity of the SPIRIT in the bond of peace." (Ephesians 4:3)

Over the past five years much has been accomplished, most of which has been summarized/reported in our weekly Church MIRROR, so I, not boasting but humbled by GOD's blessings, summarize some of the accomplishments as a reminder that by GOD's favor in a place, we have come a long way. There have been large growth in our membership, and the number of ministers called, licensed and ordained (total 6). Additions through training/teaching have included deacons, trustees, ushers, and choirs. Growth has also come through community and outreach services/ activities such as our strategic partnership activities with the Church at Grace Park (a partnership which greatly led us into the community with our kindness blitzes, and in world-wide TV exposure by being awarded the Church of the Week by the 700 Club, the Jericho Covenant (uniting four churches in outreach activities and improved human relations, etc.) the Fort Campbell military, the Fort Campbell Community Church and our church's $20,000.00 recent gift to Fisk University. We opened our doors to various community entities such as NAACP, Omega Psi Fraternity "Ques for Christ" revivals, DeWitt Johnson and Touching the World's TV broadcasts, and the meetings at our church with Tying Nashville Together, The Operation Andrews Group, the Red Cross and Life Screening organizations, the anger/management/counseling/youth programs led by our deacons,, Volunteer Mass Choir rehearsals, the Vanderbilt University Non-Smoking program, Wellness and Health related seminars/forums, the Backfield in Motion program for homeless men, scholarships and donations to Tennessee State University, Fisk University, American Baptist College, the IMF MLK scholarships and church scholarships to members. Local school outreach included our Salvation Army (Football) support program and seasonal baskets to needy families, gifts and money to our Mothers-Babies project with Meharry Medical College, books to Mckissack School Library, and collected and mailed gifts to Africa. We instituted the recognition of the Unsung Community Heroes program, and expanded our volunteer services at the Church at Grace Park, our singing groups at other churches, our church visitations throughout the community. We have received awards, plaques, and other recognitions by several groups such as internationally known Bobby Jones, the Omega Psi Fraternity, the NAACP, the military at Fort Campbell, etc. Our church has been invited, and we have preached at other churches as well as invited to come here. All this and more in addition to our regular pastoral and other duties for internal ministries through benevolence, personal and group counseling, visits to members or relatives, baby dedications, funerals here and elsewhere, etc. We paid off the roof debt and operate months with a tiny surplus.

We are a loving, giving, and nurturing church family and I thank GOD for it all. Your sacrificial gifts and your presence and graciousness given throughout whenever called have made us a beacon of light in this community, whereof I am glad. I am also appreciative for our time together. *"I will praise the LORD as long as I live."* (Psalm 146:2)

In response to GOD's call to go, at the end of July 31, 2008, I must leave you having been blessed by you and the FATHER in heaven. *"To those who have been called, who are loved by GOD the FATHER, and kept by JESUS, mercy peace and love be yours in abundance"*, said Jude in Jude 1:1-2.

I commend you to GOD, the FATHER, JESUS CHRIST the Son and the Holy Spirit and pray that **"the BEST IS YET to COME."**

Yours in Christian love,

Reverend Dr. Alvin E. Miller, Sr., Pastor

A Farewell Reception honoring Reverend Miller and Mrs. Dominique Miller for their five years of faithful service as Pastor and First Lady was held Saturday, July 21-25 in the church fellowship hall.

In following Reverend Miller's resignation, the church carried on, holding regular morning worship services as well as several special evening worship services. The Layman League held its annual Prayer Breakfast on Saturday, July 13. The guest preacher was Reverend Corey Schull, pastor of First Baptist Church in Campbellsville, Kentucky. Deacon Bernard Sparks was Master of Ceremonies, scripture was read by Deacon Harry Barnett, music was provided by Trustee Louis King, and Trustee Preston Mitchell introduced the speaker, Reverend Howard Jones, pastor of Fairfield Baptist Church. Brother Tim Warfield was chairman of breakfast preparations, and Deacon Harry Barnett was set-up chairman.

Pleasant Green celebrated its 123rd Homecoming Celebration on July 26 honoring all members with 50 plus years of membership, and living legacies of Pleasant Green's history that are still members of the church. A special article appeared in The Nashville Pride newspaper, featuring honoree Brother Joseph Herrod, who was a descendant of our first pastor, Reverend William Haynes.

The Layman League also sponsored a Family and Friends Day service at 3:30 PM on October 26, 2008. Dinner was provided in the fellowship hall after morning worship service for members of Pleasant Green and our guests from Kentucky. Reverend W. Locke showcased his powerful singing skills along with the Male Chorus from Elevated Baptist Church.

Chapter Seven

A Time for Rebuilding

On September 7, 2008, the Deacon Ministry called a church information meeting to share plans for the operation of the church and its ministries in the absence of a pastor. A Pulpit Supply Committee was formed consisting of Deacons Roxie Johnson, Charles Gillespie, and Sister Latosha Warfield. Their task was to complete the weekly worship participants' roster. They asked members for the names of persons who wished to participate in a leadership role in the Sunday Worship service, and the names of persons to serve as guest speakers. The following ministers served as guest speakers for the remainder of the year:

Reverends Samella Junior-Spence, Pierre Moss, Dana Forrest, Edith Kimbrough,

Inman Otey, Pastor of New Zion Jerusalem Church; Jimmy Duggans, Jr., Elder at Mt. Zion Baptist Church, Moses Msihi, Associate Minister, First Baptist Church, Capitol Hill;

Odie Hoover, pastor of Greater Grace Baptist Church, and James Brigham, Elder at Mt. Zion Baptist Church.

Some ministers, like Reverend Hoover and Reverend Brigham, were so well received by the congregation that they served as guest speakers for an entire month, except first Sundays, which were generally led by Rev. Dr. Spence.

On Sunday, September 28, an informational meeting was held after the morning worship service. It was announced that on the third Sundays in succeeding months, beginning in October, there would be informational meetings after church. All members were asked to mark their calendars and remain after service for those meetings.

On Sunday, October 19, 2008, the church elected five members to serve on the Pastoral Search Committee. Sixteen candidates were nominated. The members who received the highest number of votes were: Reverend Evelyn Barbour, Trustee Henrietta McCallister, Deacon Richard Friley, Brother Kenneth Mckay, and Brother Theodore Lewis. Ex-officio members were: Deacon Bernard Sparks, chairman of the Deacon Ministry, and Trustee Joel Dobbins, chairman of the Trustee Ministry.

On October 28, the Deacon Ministry held a meeting in the church fellowship hall. The Deacons unanimously agreed to ask the church to pray for our church and especially the Pastor's Search Committee. Fasting also became a part of the request. Every member (wherever they were) was asked to pray at 12:00 noon each Tuesday, and at 6:00 PM each Wednesday. These special prayers were under the leadership of Reverend Pierre Moss at noon and Deacon Cordelia Wakefield at 6:30PM.

2009 was a year that began with the inauguration of Barack Obama as the first African-American president of the United States. This historic event took place on Tuesday, January 20 in our nation's capital. Based on the numbers for attendance, television viewer-ship, and internet usage, it was among one of the most observed events by a global audience ever.

As African-Americans across the nation were basking in joy and pride over the newly elected President of the United States, the members of Pleasant Green began taking the necessary steps to secure a new leader, while maintaining the stability of its regularly scheduled meetings and worship services. During the early months of 2009 the Pulpit Supply Committee continued to utilize ministers who were already members of the church.. As the year progressed the list of ministers expanded to include ministers and associate ministers from other area churches. Those ministers included:

Rev. James Shelton, - Cleveland Street Baptist Church

Rev. Inman Otey- Zion New Jerusalem Church

Rev. Odie Hoover- Grace Covenant Church

Rev. Marvin Neal- Westwood Baptist Church

Rev. Emmanuel Reid- Mt. Gilead Baptist Church

Rev. James Brigham- Mt. Zion Baptist Church

Rev. Michael Lomax- Fifteenth Avenue Baptist Church

Rev. Darius Butler- Fifteenth Avenue Baptist Church

During this same time period the Pastor's Search Committee was busy establishing the criteria that the congregation wanted for the next pastor of Pleasant Green. Their first source of information for this criteria was the Holy Bible. They utilized and emphasized the following importance of the scripture: 1Timothy 3:2-7 (KJV)

1. *This is a true saying. If a man desire the office of bishop, he desireth a good work...*
2. *A bishop then must be blameless, the husband of one wife, vigilant, sober, of good behavior, given to hospitality; apt to teach*
3. *Not given to wine, no striker, not greedy or filthy lucre; but patient, not a brawler; not covetous;*
4. *One that ruleth well his own house, having his children in subjection with all*
5. *For if a man not know how to rule his own house, how shall he take care of the church of God?*
6. *Not a novice, lest being lifted up with pride he fall into the condemnation of the devil.*
7. *Moreover he must have a good report of them which are without; lest he fall into reproach and the snare of the devil.*

To insure that the next pastor would be a good fit for the church, a survey was administered to the congregation seeking specific qualities that they wanted in the next pastor. After administering the survey to the congregation, the search committee found that the members wanted to see these qualities in the next pastor: 1) that he be male 2) that he have a Master's Degree in theology, and 3) that marital status was not an issue

The Search Committee advertised the pastoral vacancy at Pleasant Green in local newspapers. Over one hundred applications were submitted. After weeks of analyzing applications, on-site visits to churches, matching the candidates to the criteria, the search was narrowed down to three finalists. The finalists were: Reverend James Shelton, Reverend Odie Hoover, and Reverend Darius Butler.

The Search Committee planned three weekends of special meetings between the three finalists and the congregation. These meetings occurred on successive weekends starting on Saturday, May 30, 2009, and ending on Sunday, June 13, 2009. The schedule for those meetings was as follows: On Saturday, the pastoral candidate had a meeting with the Negotiation & Search Committee, the Deacons and Trustees, and the remaining Pleasant Green congregation. Box lunches were served. On Sunday, each pastoral candidate preached his final sermon before the vote for the next pastor. This was followed by a reception in the Fellowship Hall for the candidate and his family.

The voting date for the pastoral vacancy was held on Saturday, July 18, 2009 in the church's main sanctuary using paper ballots (one vote per member). All current members who were listed on the church roster that was maintained by the church were eligible to vote. Absentee ballots were available for members who were ill, or out of town on the day of the election. The absentee ballots had to be signed and mailed to the church (postmarked by July 10) or hand-delivered to the church clerk beginning Sunday, July 12, 2009. The envelope containing the absentee ballot had to be sealed and signed across the back by the voter in order to be counted.

The candidate who received over 50% of the vote was declared as the winner. After all of the ballots were counted, the pastoral candidate who received the most votes, and was declared to be the next pastor-elect of Pleasant Green was Reverend Darius Butler.

On Sunday, August 16, 2009 Deacon Bernard Sparks called a church meeting and announced that the first choice candidate, Reverend Darius Butler, had withdrawn his name and no longer wished to be considered for the pastorate of Pleasant Green. The Pulpit Supply Committee went back to the list of previously called ministers to preach on Sundays until a new pastor could be called. Reverend Michael Lomax, one of the most popular supply ministers, preached on several Sundays during this period. He was a dynamic speaker. He received high praise after each sermon that he preached.

He also received high praise from members of his home church, Fifteenth Avenue Baptist Church. After hearing the glowing reviews of Reverend Lomax's sermons at Fifteenth

Avenue Baptist Church, Sister Madeline Barton called Reverend Lomax and asked him if he would consider submitting the necessary information to become a supply minister at Pleasant Green. His response was, "Yes".

After Reverend Butler declined the pastorate of Pleasant Green, the Search Committee was faced with the dilemma of going back through the entire search process again, or working with the supply ministers that the church had already heard. The position of the Search Committee was to start all over again, screening new applicants, listening to trial sermons, and ultimately voting on a new pastor after all steps in the process had been completed. A majority in the congregation felt that the congregation should choose from those that the congregation had already heard. Many did not want to go through the time and expense that a new search would involve. During a church meeting, Sister Beverly Barton made a motion that the search committee go back and review Reverend Lomax's file to see if he met the previously established criteria for the pastorate of Pleasant Green. Reverend Lomax's file was reviewed and it was determined that he did meet the criteria.

On Sunday, August 16, 2009 Bernard Sparks, Chairman of the Deacon Ministry, shared the following recommendation from the Deacon Ministry with the congregation:

The church should call Reverend Michael Lomax as the next pastor of Pleasant Green. The recommendation was based on the fact that the church had been without a pastor for almost a year, and it was time to have stability in the pastoral leadership of the church.

After discussion, the church unanimously agreed to call Reverend Michael Lomax as the next pastor of Pleasant Green.

After accepting the call to be the next pastor of Pleasant Green, Reverend Lomax set out to get to know the members better. He was interested in hearing their concerns and goals for the church, and he was also interested in sharing his plans and vision for the future. On Wednesday evening, September 23, Reverend Lomax met with a large portion of the congregation in the Fellowship Hall for a Chew & Chat session. During this meeting the members and Pastor learned a great deal about each other.

Not wanting to leave a stone unturned in his quest for knowledge from the members, Reverend Lomax also visited the sick and shut-in during this period. He and First Lady Tamura Lomax, along with four deacons visited those who could not come to church. Later, Reverend Lomax said that his goal was to personally visit all sick & shut-in members quarterly.

THE DAWNING OF A NEW DAY

2010 was a year in which the weather negatively affected church attendance in Nashville. In January and December many area churches including Pleasant Green cancelled Sunday morning services because of icy and snowy conditions. During the first two days of May, historic flooding took place in Nashville. Over 13 inches of rain fell in a two day period. The Cumberland River reached nearly 12 feet above flood stage before water finally began to recede. Hundreds of people had to be rescued from their homes by boat or canoes. Several families in the Pleasant Green congregation had to leave their homes for months and replace precious possessions that had been ravaged by the flood waters. Those families in the Pleasant Green congregation that were negatively affected by the flood included Ruby and Isaac Burford, Latosha and Tim Warfield, Vera and Herman Dixon, and Florence Anderson. The church provided aid to these families with money for food, shelter, and clothing. Several members in the church also assisted with the hard work of salvaging remaining possessions, and moving items to safer locations.

Despite the bad weather and its negative impact on area church services, the overall mood of the membership at Pleasant Green during 2010 was one of excited anticipation. The church had called Reverend Michael R. Lomax as its 10th pastor, and plans were underway for a momentous Installation service. The following persons served on the Installation Steering Committee:

Chairman – Walbrey Whitelow
Co-Chairman- Henry Berry
Publicity-   Loyce Thompson
Brochure/Program – Dr. Bernardeen Fleming
Correspondence/ Invitations- Dr. Edith Kimbrough
Budget – Angela Dobbins
First lady's Luncheon – Deborah Sparks
Brunch/Reception – Vivian Berry
Transportation – Richard Friley
Pastor's Pancake Breakfast – Bernard Sparks
Staging/Logistics/Decorations – Elizabeth Hester
AV Media/ photographer – Joel Dobbins
Ushers/Hosts/Hostesses/Amenities/Courtesies – Judy Sanders

The Installation Steering Committee met monthly to hear updates from the sub-committee chairs. The sub-committees listed above included nearly all of the members of the church. Everyone was excited about the installation of the new pastor, and everyone wanted to play a part in this historic occasion. The complete list of subcommittees was:

Publicity: Loyce Thompson, Chairman- Members: Washington Dobbins, Wanda Scott, Mary Hamby, Ella Thompson, Reverend Dr. Samella Spence.

Brochure/Program: Dr. Bernardeen Fleming, Chairman, Doris Dobbins, Co-Chairman- Members: Madeline Barton, Wanda Scott, DeSean Keys, Lifran Fort, Reverend Dr. Samella Spence, Beverly Barton

Correspondence/Invitations: Reverend Edith Kimbrough, Chairman- Members: Deborah Sparks, Reverend Evelyn Barbour, Rev. Dr. Samella Spence, Loyce Thompson

Budget: Angela Dobbins, Chairman- Members: Henry Stinson, Marilyn Hiner, Walbrey Lawrence, Willis McCallister, Madeline Barton

First Lady's Luncheon –Deborah Sparks, Chairman- Members: Gloria Lewis, Vivian Berry

Brunch/Reception – Vivian Berry, Chairman- Members: Marilyn Hiner, Latosha Warfield, Jennifer Johnson, Julia Moss, Herman Dixon DeSean Keys, David and Jamal Berry

Transportation/Security – Richard Friley, Chairman- Members: Louis King, Harry Barnett, Trustees (male), Deacons (male)

Pastor's Pancake Breakfast – Bernard Sparks, Chairman- Members: The Layman League, Trustees (male), Deacons (male).

Staging/logistics/Decorations: Elizabeth Hester, Chairman- Roxie Johnson, Co-Chairman Members: Lifran Fort, Michelle Lynum, Rev. Dr. Spence, Herman Brady, Harry Barnett, Faye Soloman, Helena Merritt, Tim Warfield, Michaelangelo McCallister, C.C. Johnson, Antoine Landers, David Haynes

AV Media/Photography: Joel Dobbins, Chairman- Members: Odell Moss, Washington Dobbins, Austin Wilhoite, Jordan Dobbins

Ushers/Hostesses/Amenities – Judy Sanders, Chairman- Members: Shirlyn Johnson, Antoine Landers, Faye Soloman, Tim Warfield, DeSean Keys, Tyeshia Jackson, Moni Moelups, Shanel Thompson, Marlinda Gillespie

Souvenirs: DeSean Keys, Chairman- Members: Cordelia Wakefield, Kristen Brown, Madeline Barton, Michael king

Music: Reverend Dr. Samella Spence, Pleasant Green Church Choir

Music Guests: Dr. Sherman Tribble, New Visions Baptist Choir, C.C. Johnson, Diana Poe, Keith Wilson, George Woods

Pre-Installation activities included the First Lady's Luncheon which was held at Vanderbilt Stadium Club on Saturday, March 13, 2010 and the Pancake Breakfast for Reverend Lomax, which was held that same morning in the church fellowship hall. First ladies from area churches were invited to the luncheon as special guests, and pastors from neighboring churches were invited to the Pancake Breakfast.

The Installation Service was held Sunday afternoon, March 14, 2010 in the main sanctuary. The sermon was given by Reverend Dr. William Buchanan, pastor of Fifteenth Avenue Baptist Church. The Ceremony of Installation was conducted by Reverend Dr. Forrest Harris, President of American Baptist College, and a former pastor of Pleasant Green. The Prayer of Installation was done by Reverend Brad Braxton. Special music was provided by guest soloists, Diana Poe, Kimberly Fleming, and Minister Keith Wilson from Atlanta, Georgia.

Shortly after his installation as the 10th Pastor of Pleasant Green, Reverend Lomax presented his 10 point Pastoral Vision for Pleasant Green. The scriptural basis for a Written Vision is Habakkuh" 2: 1&2." *I will stand at my watch and station myself on the ramparts; I will look to see what HE will say to me, and what answer I am to give this complaint. Then the Lord replied: Write down the revelation and make it plain on tablets so that a herald may run with it."*

Pastoral Vision

1) **Vision of Love-** The cornerstone of the church is love. The church ought to be a space for grace. If God is love, then we, who are created in the likeness of God, must reflect God's love for one another. Love is challenging because it is an embrace of that which is familiar and yet that which is foreign. That which is written and that which is from beyond our community, God's example in Jesus Christ is that kind of love. The Greatest of all three is love. (1 John 4:16/ 1Corinthians 13:13)

2) **Vision of Faith and Faithfulness-:** The church has its roots in the fundamental belief that nothing is impossible for God (hymns like "God Never Fails", "We've Come This Far by Faith" embody this belief.) Faith helps us have vision beyond our context, but it is not enough to have faith without faithfulness. Faithfulness is the commitment to do the work necessary to bring faith into focus and achieve the things which God has placed on our hearts to pursue. (Hebrews 11:6/ James 2: 17-26)

3) **Vision of Hope-** The church ought to be a place that ignites the spark of hope within our hearts. It is to this end that we pray to become a place where the congregants and the community members are affirmed. As doubts, fears, and frustrations are overcome by our new hope – the human soul is inspired to become its best self.

4) **Vision of Excellence-** God gave us an excellent gift in Jesus Christ. In response to the excellent gift we received in Jesus Christ, we ought to respond with a spirit and attitude of excellence as individuals and as a congregational community. From our personal lives outside of the church, to our professions: to our participation in worship, to ministerial programs; to our community and other – we should have in our hearts that whatever "IF" is "It" will be done to the best of our abilities. (John 1:14 / 2Corinthians 9: 15)

5) **Vision of Engagement and Involvement:** We seek to engage all aspects of our congregation/ community from the youngest members to those who are young at heart and we will be intentional not only to **engage** in conversation but create avenues to **involve** each person in the life of the congregation and community,)1 Corinthians 12:12)

6) **Vision of Edification**: The easiest thing in the world is to destroy, but it takes work and diligence to build. To edify is to build up or improve. At Pleasant Green we pray that we would be a church that provides acts of service that builds individuals, builds families, build our congregation and ultimately the community around us. Through relevant acts of service such as Room-in-the-Inn programs, counseling youth, young adult, young at heart ministries, invigorating worship, education, prayer, fellowship, the re-commissioning of our historical committee; the CDC and remaining open to what GOD has in store, we will uphold our covenant to build lives.

7) **Vision of Exchange and Empowerment-** Empowerment is not simply seeing the possibility, but galvanizing resources to make possibilities a reality. To move from seeing the possibilities to making realities, persons must have opportunities to share their narratives and exchange ideas and ideals. We seek to provide the space and the resources necessary for congregants and community members to achieve tangible goals; yet continue to envision more robust dreams. (John 1:14)

8) **Vision of Holistic Health**- We seek holistic health. We want to be a healthy body and we want the same for everyone who comes in our midst. In the church we begin with spiritual health, but we recognize that spiritual health should translate into other areas of health to include the physical, financial, emotional, psychological and educational, etc (Reference- the Gospels – Jesus addresses every aspect of the human dilemma – Luke 10:27

9) **Vision of Growth**- It is imperative that we never stop growing/ evolving. While we pray for quantitative or numerical membership growth, we simultaneously ask for growth in our love for ourselves and others, understanding of God and ourselves, growth in our character; our contributions to God and Neighbor (John 12:32)

10) **Vision of Equity and Justice** – God in the scriptures consistently demonstrates a heart for equity and justice in the world. In all of our pursuits, we should pray for equity and justice for all. Which means being heavenly minded, but acknowledging and calling attention to the social sins that negatively impact the divine dignity of all human beings the. literacy, healthcare, rights of aging, economic oppression, rights of women, etc. (Luke 4: 18)

Reverend Lomax also shared his personal Pastoral Mission which was the Action
Plan for making the 10 point {Pastoral Vision become a reality. The Pastoral Mission Plan was as follows:

1) **Love the People**- Get to know the people. Update Church Records in terms of Church Membership Census. Document all contributions of all members (not financial but gifts inventory) ministerial involvement.
2) **Learn the Processes**- Understand how, what, when and where. The relevance of the things we do and how they improve or impair our acts of service to the congregation and community. Document the process to help leadership remain clear on how we all function as one body.
3) **Listen to the Leadership and Congregation**- Bi-Annual Chat and Chews- Place them on the calendar for 2010- Beginning of the Year- Middle of the Year- before summer vacation and traveling. Quarterly or Monthly Chairs Breakfast – an intentional time with chairs of committees and Core Leadership Team to discuss visionary issues.
4) **Property Maintenance Schedule**
5) **Building our Core-** Leadership Training (based on what we want to achieve) Sunday School Training – TNLT (The Next Level Training, Grow Budget (Revenue), Hire Staff, Create and / or reconnect Communal Connections and Ministerial Fellowships/ Fisk/TSU/United Way/ Local High Schools and other community associations.
6) **Align Ministries-** to segments of the congregation (Toddlers and Tots under 5 – youth under 10-transitional youth (11-14) Future Focus Fellowship (14-18) young professional (19-35- mentor 35-70/elder 85 – to young at heart.
7) **Update By-laws** – to match our context and support a "Right Now/Beyond Now or Mirror Window" vision for ministry.
8) **Continue Weekly Conference calls-**ensure that communications and connections with ailing members are made
9) **Launch the Pleasant Green Prayer Team-** a team of people who rotate and pray on behalf of the church, the pastor and consistently cover us in prayer. Read book on prayer.
10) **Launch Pleasant Green Website-** to create a presence on the Internet to inform persons about our church virtually.

Early in the year 2010, Reverend Lomax decided to involve the congregation in an extensive assessment of the status of the church and existing programs at a Leadership Retreat with the idea of making changes where necessary. He used the Book of Nehemiah, Chapters 1-7 to provide an insider prospective of a rebuilding project similar to the one that was about to occur at Pleasant Green. In this scriptural passage, Nehemiah seeks to rebuild the deteriorating gates of Jerusalem. The scriptural passage was a helpful frame of reference in terms of rebuilding worn or torn down "gates". Reverend Lomax challenged the leadership of the church to take ownership of a gate that might need to be rebuilt. A chart with the following Ministerial Gates was presented to those in attendance. The gates for adoption included the following:

- All in the Family
- Anniversary/Homecoming
- Bible Study
- Culinary
- Children's Choir
- Christian Education
- Counseling
- CDC
- Diaconate
- Directory
- Finance Ministry
- Hospitality
- Ladies Aid
- Layman's League
- Media Ministry
- Men's Fellowship
- New Members Ministry
- Pleasant Green Prayer Team
- Pastor's Aid Prison Ministry
- Scholarship Committee
- Sunday School (as a part of Christian Education)
- Trustee Ministry
- Usher Ministry
- Vacation Bible school
- Worship
- Women's Fellowship
- Worship Music
- Website
- Youth Ministry
- Young at Heart Ministry

Reverend Lomax referenced Ecclesiastes 3- to everything there is a season…when he said, "It is time to get up and harvest." The measure of this season will be directly connected to our ability to provide sustainable "gates" or ministries that engage the heart, soul, and minds of the members of our congregation and community.

Several changes occurred at the church during 2010 as various church leaders adopted or re-opened the gates.

1) **Children's Choir**- under the direction of Ms. Beverly Barton and Ms. Madeline Barton the Children's Choir was reorganized. The children performed so well early in the year that they were given the 2nd Sunday as their regular Sunday to sing. They also performed in June in a Children's Worship Day Service and also in December in a Christmas skit called "Back to the Manger."
2) **Church Council Meetings**- were held January 23, and on April 10. A three-day planning meeting was held November 10-12.
3) **Christian Education**- Mrs. Benita McLean was named the new Christian Education Director, and a new Christian Education curriculum emerged.
4) **New Members Class**- met each Sunday during Sunday School under the leadership of Trustee Angela Dobbins, who was later assisted by Deacon Henry Berry.
5) **Website**- information about the church could now be accessed on the internet@www.pleasantgreenmbc.org. Reverend Lomax and Washington Dobbins led this effort.
6) **Weekly Leadership Tele-Conference call**- occurred each Thursday at 7:30AM between various church leaders and the pastor to receive current updates on ailing or troubled members, relevant issues and prayer.
7) **History Ministry** – under the leadership of Loyce Thompson and Wanda Scott the History Committee began having monthly meetings for the purpose of writing a 2nd history book to continue the documentation of church history for the years 2003 – 2013, and to establish a permanent location within the church for the church archives.
8) **Property Maintenance**- The Trustee Ministry led by Joel Dobbins commissioned a mold abatement/waterproofing project for the front of the building.
9) **Community Outreach**- a response was given to flood victims within the congregation and a donation to the American Red Cross was made.
10) **Media Ministry**- under the leadership of Trustee Joel Dobbins, the sound system was upgraded, new microphones were purchased, and the control panel for the sound system of the church was moved to the balcony. Later, two media screens were added to the main sanctuary.
11) **Music Ministry**- established the Worship Chorale initially under the direction of Reverend Justin Cunningham, and later Trustee Joel Dobbins.
12) **Dance Ministry**- was initiated by Reverend Lomax after the 1st Anniversary Luncheon. Kierra Gonzales provides liturgical dancing monthly during morning worship services.
13) **Model of Ministry**- Reverend Lomax presented the following Model of Ministry as the new organizational structure of the church.

Model of Ministry

Congregational Care

Building Community

Youth

Christian Education

Relationship With God through His son Jesus Worship

Open the Gates
CDC
Strategic
Communal
Affairs

Elders

Adults

Building Community

PLEASANT GREEN

THE DAWNING OF A NEW DAY

AT
PLEASANT GREEN
MISSIONARY BAPTIST CHURCH
FOUNDED IN 1885

WITH
THE INSTALLATION
OF
THE REVEREND
MICHAEL R. LOMAX,
M.DIV. / M.B.A.

THE SERVICE OF INSTALLATION AT
FOURTEEN TEN JEFFERSON STREET, NASHVILLE, TENNESSEE
ON SUNDAY, MARCH FOURTEENTH, TWO THOUSAND TEN
AT FOUR O'CLOCK IN THE AFTERNOON

"LOVE, LISTEN, LIVE AND LET GOD"

About Our Pastor

Reverend Michael R. Lomax, M.Div./M.B.A.

Michael is the youngest of four children born to Joe and Kathryn Lomax of Platteville, Wisconsin. He could have never imagined the plans God had for his life. In 1996, Michael was called into the ministry. His call came in the form of a dream where God revealed to him through Ephesians 4:1-15 his thesis of ministry. Every day Michael tries to live out this three part thesis: to walk worthy of the call, to teach and to preach Jesus Christ.

In his primary years he was consistently confronted with the issues of racial tension. As the only African-American in his entire elementary school, he could identify with W.E.B. DuBois' statement written in the classic narrative *The Soul of Black Folk*, "How does it feel to be a problem?...One ever feels the two-ness, an American, a Negro, two souls, two thoughts, two un-reconciled strivings, two warring ideals in one dark body." It was this sense of warring ideals that his call was not just to preach salvation, but also to preach about hope, love, social consciousness and self analysis offered in the Gospel of Jesus Christ.

In 1994, Michael graduated Cum Laude from Morehouse College in Atlanta, Georgia with a B.A. in Business Management. He went on to work for Wachovia Bank in their Management Rotational Program. In 1996, Michael was hired by Nations Bank as a Manager of a Financial Center. With grace and determination, Michael was granted numerous promotions and at the age of 26 was promoted to the Executive Leadership team for Bank of America in the Mid-South Region of the Consumer Bank as a Consumer Market Manager/Vice President. In 2000, he left Bank of America to pursue his ministerial call and to assist his pastor in the development of a $10 million church growth initiative.

In January of 2001, Michael was licensed to preach the Gospel of Jesus Christ. In the fall of the same year, he enrolled in seminary at Candler School of Theology, Emory University. In May 2004, he completed his Master's of Divinity with a special emphasis in Black Church Studies. Michael was further honored by the academic leadership of the seminary when he was selected as the 2004 John Owen Smith Award recipient. This award is presented by the faculty in recognition of the senior M. Div student who is best able to communicate the Gospel faithfully and imaginatively through preaching. An honor that he is very proud of, but prays he upholds every time he approaches the preaching moment.

Michael went on to further study, enrolling into the accelerated One Year MBA program at the Goizueta Business School, Emory University. He graduated in May of 2005 with an MBA, with a concentration in Strategy and Management Consulting. In August, he and his family relocated to Nashville, TN where they joined Fifteenth Avenue Baptist Church. On his birthday, October 22, 2006, Michael's call to ministry was affirmed by his Fifteenth Avenue Church Family as he was ordained by his spiritual mentor and Pastor, Reverend Dr. William F. Buchanan. This day will forever be etched in his memory as confirmation that he was created for God's service.

Michael enjoys the bliss of marriage with his best friend, love of his life and college sweetheart, the former Ms. Tamura Gainey. The two married in 1997 and have been blessed by God with two wonderful sons, Michael Leroy and Martin Joseph. Michael is a Managing Director/Group Vice President for SunTrust Bank in Private Wealth Management and leads the Wealth team for the Nashville Market. Michael is an aspiring author recently contributing to a liturgical entry in the African Pulpit 's Online Lectionary Series called "A Service of Healing.

Throughout the years Michael has acquired many titles and initials: Teacher, Preacher, Reverend, Morehouse Man, Executive, Strategist, Investment Advisor, M. Div, MBA, etc., however, the titles he is most proud-are the ones often overlooked: husband, father, friend and servant of Jesus Christ.

The Order of Service

THE ORGAN PRELUDE
    Reverend Dr. Sherman R. Tribble
    Reverend Dr. Samella W. Junior Spence

THE SEATING OF THE FIRST FAMILY

THE PROCESSIONAL .... The Dais

THE CALL TO WORSHIP .... Reverend Dr. Edith W. Kimbrough
Pleasant Green Missionary Baptist Church

The HYMN .... Mass Choir and Congregation
"All Hail the Power" (James Ellor)

THE INVOCATION .... The Fleming Family
"The Lord's Prayer" (arr.)

THE SCRIPTURE
    Old Testament Reading .... Reverend Christophe Ringer
Pastor, Howard Congregational Church
    New Testament Reading .... Reverend Andrew Hunt
Pastor, Transformation Church
Chicago, IL

THE ANTHEM .... Mass Choir
"Praise Ye Jehovah" (Glenn L. Jones)

THE WELCOME .... Sister Nannie Parker Fort
Centenarian, Pleasant Green Baptist Church

THE MINISTRY OF GIVING .... Trustee, Dr. Henrietta McCallister
    Offertory Music
    Offertory Prayer .... Deacon Washington Dobbins, Jr.

THE INTRODUCTION OF THE SPEAKER .... Sister Ella Thompson

THE MUSIC OF INSPIRATION .... Mrs. Diana Poe
Fifteenth Avenue Baptist Church

THE SERMON .... Reverend Dr. William F. Buchanan
Pastor, Fifteenth Avenue Baptist Church

THE INVITATION TO DISCIPLESHIP . . . . Reverend Dr. William Buchanan

THE HYMN OF INVITATION . . . . Choir and Congregation
"Lead Me, Guide Me" (Doris Akers)

THE INTRODUCTION OF INSTALLATION OFFICIANT . . . . Reverend Pierre Moss
Pleasant Green Baptist Church

THE CEREMONY OF INSTALLATION . . . . Reverend Dr. Forrest Harris
President, American Baptist College

The Charge to the Minister
The Charge to the Congregation
The Church's Response . . . . The Congregation
(Audience Stand)

As brothers and sisters in Christ, we accept our responsibility
to advance the word and the work of the kingdom of God.

As partners in the Covenant of Faith, we affirm our commitment
to be dutiful stewards of our time, our talents, and our possessions.

As a church family, we honor our promise to love and provide for our
shepherd, to encourage and support his ministry in this church and
in this community. To God be the glory and dominion forever
and ever. Amen! Amen!

The Prayer of Installation . . . . Reverend Dr. Brad Braxton

The Music. . . . . Mass Choir
"Order My Steps" Mrs. Angie Clark, Soloist

THE INVESTITURE . . . . Reverend Dr. Forrest Harris
The Robe: . . . . Rev. Dr. Samella W. Junior Spence and Tamura Lomax, M.Div/Th.M
The Bible: . . . . Reverend Evelyn Barbour, Michael L. Lomax and Martin J. Lomax
The Keys: . . . . Trustee Joel Dobbins, LaPrecious Wilkerson and Eriqua Martin

THE MUSIC . . . . Minister, Keith Wilson
Atlanta, GA

THE PASTOR'S REMARKS . . . . Reverend Michael Lomax

THE CLOSING MUSIC . . . . . . *"Wherever I Go"* . . . . Mass Choir
Dr. Michael Lindsey, Director

THE BENEDICTION . . . . Reverend Dr. William Buchanan

You are invited to join us for a reception in the Fellowship Hall

Pictorial Highlights

of the

INSTALLATION — INVESTITURE SERVICES

For the

TENTH PASTOR
REVEREND MICHAEL R. LOMAX, M.DIV/M.B.A.

Reverend Lomax receives the charge from the minister

Reverend Lomax receives the Bible from Reverend Evelyn Barbour

The prayer of installation

Reverend lomax receives congratulations from family and friends

First Lady's Luncheon at Vanderbilt Stadium Club
Saturday, March 13, 2010

First Lady Tamura Lomax

State Representative Brenda Gilmore presents a proclamation plaque to First Lady Tamura Lomax

NEW DIRECTIONS FOR THE CHURCH

2011 was the year when the royal wedding between Prince William and Kate Middleton captivated the nation. It was also the year in which Bill Haslam was elected as governor of Tennessee. Locally, it was a time when the Jeff Fisher era with the Titans ended as the new coach, Mike Munchak was hired.

At Pleasant Green the year began on a positive note. An organizational structure for the church was in place. The quarterly Leadership Council meetings continued with church leaders divided into not five council areas to plan activities for the next quarters.. Members became excited when they were able to hear plans for upcoming events for the church that fit into the Model for Ministry.

Bible study was expanded to offer multiple class offerings on Wednesday nights. The new classes included: The Book of Ester – (in the main sanctuary), Doctrinal Study- (in the 3rd floor Music room), and Children and Youth Studies – choir rehearsal, Bible study, refreshments- (in the Fellowship Hall).

Deacon Henry Berry also presented a seminar for teens, which lasted several weeks entitled, "The 7 Habits of Highly Effective Teens". The purpose of the seminar was to provide teens with a step-by-step guide to help them improve their self-image, build friendships, resist peer pressure, and achieve goals. The information was so helpful that adults also attended the seminar.

A Christian Education Retreat was held on July 2, 2011 under the leadership of Christian Education Director, Benita Mclean. The guest lecturer was her father, Dr. Walter Sims, Pastor of Mt. Zion Baptist Church in Birmingham, Alabama. One of the outcomes of the retreat was the development of plans for increasing the number of people in attendance at Sunday school each Sunday. "Super Sunday School Day" was planned for August 7. All members of the church were strongly encouraged to attend a Sunday School class at Pleasant Green on this day. Prior to this day, members were asked to sign pledge cards indicating the Sundays that they definitely planned to attend Sunday School.

The Ministry of Music expanded to include the formation of a new Worship Chorale under the direction of Reverend Justin Cunningham. The Worship Chorale planned to sing contemporary gospel music accompanied by an ensemble of musicians which included the following: C.C. Johnson, saxophone; Joel Dobbins, bass guitar; Jordan Dobbins, drums, Doug Devlin, Reverend. Cunningham, keyboard; and on select occasions Michael Lomax, Jr. on drums.

2011 was also a time when the congregation expanded with the addition of new members. These new members included Felicia Hicks, Candace Moss, Derrick Plummer, Rene Ruffin, Keisi Williams, and former member, Karen Johnson. A New Members' Fellowship Dinner, sponsored by the Deacon Ministry and the Ladies Aid Society, was held on October 16 in the Fellowship Hall. The purpose of the dinner was for the new members and church leaders to get-acquainted with each other. Angela Dobbins, the teacher of the New Members' class, introduced each new member. Each of the church leaders, who were present, briefly explained the ministry or organization that they chaired. The hope was that the new members would join one or more organizations, and thus become active participants in the activities of the church.

The Room-in-the Inn continued, completing its 25th consecutive season. The Room-in-the Inn staff of Pleasant Green received the following letter of commendation from Charles Strobel, Founding Director of the Room-in-the-Inn program:

During November 1, 2011 to March, 2011, Pleasant Green was one of 177 congregations who gave time, talent, and service. Our members volunteered as drivers, cooks, servers of needs, shoppers for food, and washers of laundry. At the end of the season the Room-in-the-Inn volunteers went back to their houses, and the homeless guests went back to the streets of Nashville. Even though they went their separate ways, a connection between the volunteers and guests was made. This was a connection born of the mutual respect and the recognition of a common humanity. Room-in-the-Inn along with other area churches helped provide 30,000 beds, 60,000 meals, 30,000 sacked lunches, and 23,000 showers.

2011 also included many special church services that underscored the positive, upbeat mood of the congregation. One of the most joyous occasions was the celebration of Reverend Lomax's First Anniversary as the pastor of Pleasant Green. The festivities began with the First Anniversary Luncheon, which was held at Inspiration Center in Metro Center on March 26. The theme of the luncheon was "The Leader for the Times"- Bridging Gaps and Building Lives by the Power of the Holy Spirit. (Joel: 2-28-29; Acts2:17-18). The luncheon featured greetings from Wanda Scott; scripture, Theodore Lewis; invocation, Kana Gaines; solo, Andreas Hathaway, and a praise dance from Karen Gozales. Oral tributes to Pastor Lomax were rendered by Jordan Dobbins, Marlinda Gillespie, and Henry Stinson. The Mistress of Ceremonies was Dr. Belinda Lee. Doris Dobbins served as chairperson for the event.

The First Anniversary Celebration continued on Sunday, March 27 with the Reverend Andrew Hunt, Jr., pastor of Transformations Church in Chicago, Illinois as the guest speaker. Minister Keith Wilson provided special music for the service.

Education Achievement Sunday, which was observed on the 4th Sunday in May, focused on the academic accomplishments of many church members who had graduated from various educational institutions. The 2011 list of graduates included:

*Dr. Tamura Lomax- PhD- Religion- Vanderbilt University
Benita McLean – M.A Curriculum and Instruction-Trevecca University
Rev. Pierre Moss- B.A. Pastoral Studies- American Baptist College
Mylea Maria Gilmore- Diploma- Nashville Christian School
Rev. Evelyn Barbour – M.A. Religion- Emmanuel Bible College
Franchetta Greer – B.A. Speech/Communications- Public Relations – TSU
Briana Gillespie- Diploma – Nashville School of the Arts
David Jon Walker- M.A. Graphic Design- University of Memphis
Whitney Lee- B.S. Marketing (Cum laude) – Alabama A&M
Rev. Samella Spence- Th.D.-Doctor of Ministry- United Theological College
* First Lady

The Ladies Aid Society held their Annual Prayer Breakfast on Saturday, October 27 in the Church Fellowship Hall. This year the members of the Ladies Aid Society chose not to have a guest speaker. They decided to focus on prayer instead. Fervent prayers were offered by Reverends Moss, McCormick, and Kimbrough. A record turnout of 90+ guests attended the event filling the Fellowship Hall to capacity. Upon leaving, many guests stated that they enjoyed the focus on prayer, could have heard even more prayers, and looked forward to attending next year.

The Ladies Aid also held their Annual Day Service on May 20, 2012, celebrating their 60th year anniversary. This years' anniversary celebration was a musical salute to Fisk University and the Fisk Jubilee Singers. The honoree for the service was Dr. Matthew Kennedy, former Director of the Fisk Jubilee Singers. Additional guests included the following former Fisk Jubilee Singers: Debra Tillery, Kimberly Fleming, Erskine Lytle, and Teresa Hannah. Reverend James Sawyers, a fifth former Jubilee singer, delivered the sermonic meditation. The choirs of First Baptist Church, Capitol Hill, and Mt. Nebo Baptist Church also rendered musical selections. The Ladies Aid Society was pleased to present Fisk University with a check for $1500.00 from the proceeds of this program.

In December 2011 the Children's Choir presented a Christmas play entitled "The Great Christmas Giveaway, the Gift Goes On". . In addition to the children, the cast of the play also included Mr. Charles Gillespie, and Mrs. Aggie Loyal, soloist. Their participation in the play helped to "Bridge the Gaps" (of age) in casting the play.

In February of 2012 the History and Archives Committee held the Dedication Service of the newly completed Archive room. The room features large 11x 17 photographs of the 10 pastors who were called and installed at Pleasant Green. Those pastors include: Reverend William Haynes (1885- 1901), Reverend John Charles Fields (1901-1937), Reverend Samuel James (1937- 1940), Reverend Isaiah Henderson (1941-1943), Reverend Andrew L. Porter (1944 -1982), Reverend Frederick G. Sampson III ,(1983-1986), Reverend Ralph G. Henley (1986 – 1988), Reverend Dr. Forrest E. Harris (1900 – 1999), Reverend Dr. Alvin Miller (2003- 2008), Reverend Michael Lomax (2009-2012). The room also features the original pulpit chairs from the original church which was built in 1886. Pictures of people and events which cover the 121 years of the church history line the walls of the room. The History and Archives Committee includes the following members:

- Loyce Thompson – Chairperson
- Wanda Scott- Co-Chairperson
- Beverly Barton
- Madeline Barton
- Henry Berry
- Ruby Burford
- Doris Dobbins
- LiFran Fort
- Theodora Howell
- Walbrey Whitelow
- Nannie P. Fort, Historian

Mrs. Nannie Parker Fort, our church historian, and oldest member at 103, was also honored on this day with an oral tribute for her many years of service in the area of church history by Mrs. Loyce Thompson, History Committee Chairperson. Mrs. Fort also received a framed certificate and a bouquet of yellow roses.

One month later on the fourth Sunday in March the congregation celebrated the 2nd anniversary of Reverend Lomax as pastor of Pleasant Green. At the pastor's request, the celebration was simple including only a morning worship service and reception. The speaker for the morning service was Reverend Darius Butler, pastor of Tabernacle Community Baptist Church in Milwaukee, Wisconsin. Minister Keith Wilson provided special music for the service. A reception for Reverend Lomax and his family followed the morning service. During the reception Reverend Lomax and his family talked informally with the assembled guests. Pictures of the reception were taken by Deacon Roxie Johnson.

Deacon Charles Gillespie was honored with a community award for his work with youth in the area of athletics. Deacon Gillespie received a plaque, and had many of his student athletes and their families were present in the congregation to witness him receiving this award.

One month later at the conclusion of the First Sunday service in April, Reverend Lomax announced to the congregation his plans to resign as pastor of Pleasant Green. He indicated that he would be leaving the ministry entirely, and devoting his time to his family and another job in the banking industry in Richmond, Virginia. Many in the congregation were shocked, stunned, and saddened. Several dabbed at tears in their eyes. Reverend Lomax was a popular, well liked pastor. The members felt a tremendous loss with this announcement. During his statement of resignation, Reverend Lomax indicated that his last day as Pastor of Pleasant Green would be the 2nd Sunday in May, Mother's Day.On the 2nd Sunday in May, Reverend Lomax and his family were presented with tributes from several people in the congregation.

Reverend Lomax wrote the following letter of appreciation to the congregation, which appeared in the Church Mirror on this Sunday:

Pastor to People – In Appreciation

My Dearest Church Family:

I am writing today to express my deepest gratitude and sincerest thanks for three of the most wonderful years of my life – years shared as your Pastor, and yes, years of growth, love, friendship, teamwork, and much more – walking together, learning and working toward bridging gaps and building lives by the Holy Spirit.

Strange as it may seem, yet most fitting though I did not plan it that way, GOD has permitted my last Sunday with you to be Mother's Day. GOD is so awesome. Who knows better than a mother what it means to see her children grow from dependency and immaturity to independence and maturity and then leave the nest to go to college or go on to a new location for a job? It is both – a mixture of sadness and joy – sadness when the loved one physically leaves, but joy to see that good things are in store in the days to come. That somewhat describes where I am today.

Your generosity, Your graciousness, your many expressions and acts of kindness, your calls, your prayers, your words of encouragement – everything that so many of you have shared – continue to overwhelm my family and especially me. Words are limited and fail to express what we feel, yet that is what we use to let each other know just how appreciative we are for the sharing. Thank you!

I am beginning to see how Abraham must have felt when GOD summoned him to take his family and move to a new land. Such has been my call, yet there is a big difference. Abraham was to leave without returning, looking back. We have become a family and developed everlasting friendship. We love you, and you have shared your love and friendship with us. We have built ties that bind, and while I am officially no longer your Pastor, I will always be a friend, son, and permanent family member of Pleasant Green Missionary Baptist Church.

I encourage you now to love one another, pray for one another, listen to one another; share with one another; support one another, and trust one another and build bridges for each other. Keep CHRIST as the center and let the Holy Spirit guide you all things. Remember that GOD is Omnipotent, and Omnipresent. He is ALWAYS with us to lead us, to guide us and bind us together.

In closing, I pronounce the same blessing upon you that Moses was instructed by God to pronounce upon the people of Israel in the book of Numbers chapter 6 verse 23(b) – 27
(with slight interpretative effect): God spoke to Michael and said, "This is how you are to bless Pleasant Green. Say to them, "The Lord bless you and keep you: The Lord make his face to shine upon you and be gracious to you: the LORD turn his face toward you and give you peace." So thy will put my name on Pleasant Green Missionary Baptist Church, and I will bless them."

Yours In Christ,
Michael R. Lomax, Pastor

Though the congregation was saddened by the departure of Reverend Lomax as Pastor of Pleasant Green, they felt that congratulations were appropriate for a job well done. The congregation was grateful and thankful for the following:

Gates Re-opened- Developed
Church membership increase
Increased intergenerational involvement
Church Council meetings
Church Ministries restructured
Church Leadership roles defined
Church Membership Handbook developed
Church Fellowships restructured
Church Website
Church library-computers
New Church Archives developed/ dedicated
New church stationary
Church publication (Mirror) updated
Church Administrative Leaders/roles updated
Updated blended worship services
Updated Bible Study activities
Church 2-Day Seminar/Training/Planning
Children's Choir Activities
Youth outings and activities
Annual Christmas Play
Annual Easter Cantatas
History Committee re-activated
New Member Orientation Classes
Weekly Leadership Conference Call
Weekly Prayer ministry Conference Call
Weekly Worship Council
Church Outreach- Flood Victims/ Donations to Red Cross
Church Membership in Urban League
New Sunday School Study materials
Major Church Repairs and Renovations
Quarterly Member Visitations
Worship Song Leader and Worship Chorale
Church Assistant Pastor name
Church Audit re-instated

A Period of Discernment

After the resignation of Reverend Lomax, the church was once again without a pastor. Upon leaving, Reverend Lomax left several recommendations for a smooth transition. These recommendations included the following:

1) The church should pause for a period of discernment. During this time the members were urged to fast and pray on a regular basis. They were also urged to give serious thought to the qualities and qualifications that they wanted in their next pastor. This period of discernment should last for approximately six months.
2) After the period of discernment was over, a new Pastor's Search Committee should be formed that would be intergenerational. That is, the ages of the members of this committee should range from teenage years and above.

On Saturday, August 3, 2012, a church business meeting was held in the Fellowship Hall of the church to discuss future plans for the church. Several committees were formed during this meeting to help carry out the goals of the church during the remaining months of transition. The committees that were formed included :

1) A Pastor's Search Nominating Committee including the following members:
Deborah Sparks, Loyce Thompson, and Franchetta Greer
2) A Membership Handbook Committee including the following members:
Samella Spence, Angela Dobbins, Carmelia Cammon-Tate, Deborah Sparks, Walbrey Whitelow, and Marilyn Hiner
3) A Pastoral Covenant (Contract) Committee including the following members:
Julia Moss, Deborah Sparks, Wanda Scott, Theodore Lewis, and Roxie Johnson

Deacon Henry Berry, who had also been serving as Chairman of the Trustee Board, provided a revised list of members of the Trustee Board. The revised list included: Madeline Barton, Isaac Burford, Kimberly Cannon, Angela Dobbins, Joel Dobbins, Louis King, Jr., Henrietta McCallister, Preston Mitchell, Julia Moss, and Latosha Warfield. Trustees Emeritus included: Kenneth McKay, Willis McCallister, George Jemison, and Theodore Lewis.

A motion was made to accept the revised list of names as members of the Trustee Board of Pleasant Green Baptist Church. The motion carried by a show of hands of the majority of people in attendance.

Trustee Angela Dobbins provided an update on the status of discussion with Citizen's Bank about a loan for church renovations. On this day, the documentation for the loan request had not been submitted to the bank. After explaining the need for additional repairs on the church, the amount of money that the church needed to borrow was increased from $50,000.00 to $100,000.00. A motion was made to accept the recommendation from the Trustee Board to increase the amount of money to be borrowed. The motion passed by a show of hands of those in attendance.

On Sunday, November 7, 2012, a Pastor's Search Committee was elected by secret ballot. The newly elected Pastor's Search Committee included the following members: Richard Friley, Beverly Barton, Jennifer Johnson, DeSean Keys, Michaelangelo McCallister, and Gloria Lewis (alternate). The Ex-Officio members were Deacon Bernard Sparks and Trustee Kimberly Cannon.

The Search Committee started working immediately. They set a regular meeting time for Mondays @ 5:30PM, and elected officers. The officers were:

Richard Friley- Chairman
Beverly Barton- Vice Chairman
Jennifer Johnson- Secretary
DeSean Keys- Keeper of Records

They also drafted a flyer announcing the Pastoral Vacancy at Pleasant Green. The Search Committee sought input from the congregation on the qualities that they wanted in a pastor by administering two surveys. The second survey was administered because of a low number of returned surveys from survey #1 The following Resume Checklist emerged from the two surveys that were administered:

RESUME CHECKLIST
1. No desired age preference
2. Master's degree (Bachelor's Degree Survey #1)
3. 1-5 years of Pastoral Experience
4. No preference- size of current congregation
5. Married
6. Important Strengths: Preaching and Leadership
7. Activities allocated throughout the week: Administration, Visiting members in homes/ nursing homes
8. Make changes in the following areas: More contemporary and traditional music
9. Preaching style Narrative (#1), Logical, Personal, Textual (#2)
10. Top three priorities of incoming pastor: Building relationships, Leadership Vision, Evangelism, Prayer, Discipleship, Servant Leader
11. Top Three character traits: Faithful, High Integrity, Sound financial background
12. Prefer a clear calling to the ministry
13. Mix of Pastoral/ Denominational experience

The deadline to receive applicants' applications was November 26, 2012. After the deadline had passed for receiving applications, the Search Committee requested the months of December and January for reviewing applications. The prospective candidates were scheduled to preach on the 2nd, 3rd, and 4th Sundays in February and March. The projected month of selecting the next pastor was April, 2013.

On Saturday, February 9, a church business meeting was held in the Fellowship Hall. During this meeting the Pastoral Search Committee presented the name of E. Christopher Jackson, D .Min as their recommendation for the pastoral vacancy at Pleasant Green. The committee chair, Richard Friley, stated that the search committee had reviewed the resumes of 14 candidates, but that Rev. Dr. Jackson was the only one who met all of the previously established criteria. After discussion a motion was made to accept only one name, Rev. Dr. E. Christopher Jackson.

The Trustee Board also submitted a written report summarizing decisions that had been made by the Trustee Board during its 2012 quarter meetings. A physical capital needs assessment (PCNA) was done, which resulted in a list of several areas of the church that are in need of repair. The results of the Physical Capital Needs Assessment were as follows:

1) Two new A/C Gas Furnace Systems are needed on the 3rd floor
2) Flaking, loose & falling interior paint on walls, ceilings, repaired interior woodwork
3) Windows (31 Wood Frames- scrape, paint, caulk, putty
4) Metal doors: scrape, prime, paint
5) Handrails (fronts and sides)
6) Gable at front entrance (exterior)
7) Three Awnings (exterior)
8) Water damage areas throughout the building (repair, prime, and paint)
9) Roof vent

10) Installation of a chain link fence for the parking lot
11) Enlarging and remodeling the kitchen area
12) Removing old dining room floor and adding new tiles
13) New ceiling tiles for dining room area
14) New curtains for the sanctuary

Various members of the Trustee Board were charged with gathering estimates of the cost of the proposed repairs. Several companies were contacted and estimates were provided to the Trustee Board. The companies that were contacted included: Lee Company, JP's Heating & Cooling, Hiller Cooperation .Richard McKnight Carpentry/Home Repairs, Interstate AC Service, MyBran Home services, K&C Fence Company, Thornton & Associates, Inc., and Dawkins Contracting.

The Trustee Report stated that $100,000.00 was needed to complete the listed repairs. This amount had been approved at an earlier church business meeting. In a recent discussion with bank officials at Citizen's Bank, the loan is expected to be approved. Upon receipt of the mortgage proceeds the Trustee Board will contact the companies that they believe will complete the work in the most professional manner.

During this period of transition, the morale of the church was understandably low after the resignation of Reverend Lomax in May, 2012. Attendance at church, Sunday school, and Bible Study dropped off significantly. It was painful on many Sundays to see large numbers of empty pews. The number of people to join the church during this time was also low.

In an effort to bolster the spirituality of many in the church, The Ladies Aid Society decided to host a Fall Revival in November 2012. Sister Theodora Howell had heard about a young, dynamic preacher who was preaching to a packed church each Sunday. After several visits to this pastor's church, Sister Howell came back to the Ladies Aid members with a glowing report. Several other members of the Ladies Aid Society also went to hear this dynamic preacher. After these visits, the consensus among those who had heard him was to invite this pastor to Pleasant Green to lead a revival. With approval from the Deacon Board, an invitation was made. The evangelist was the Reverend John R. Faison, Sr., Pastor of Watson Grove Baptist Church. The theme for the revival was "Spiritual Renewal Through Transition". The revival was held nightly and was a huge success, bringing members of our congregation and the community together for three nights of spiritually uplifting messages and music.

The Ladies Aid Society also hosted its Annual Prayer Breakfast in October 2012, and a special Appreciation Service for Reverend Dr. Samella Spence in December 2012. The appreciation service was originally intended to be an extension of a regular Ladies Aid Society meeting, but because an overwhelming number of other church members wanted to attend this event, an invitation was extended to the whole church. It was an enjoyable time for all in attendance. These special services did much to lift the spirits of the congregation during this period of transition.

A NEW SEASON AT PLEASANT GREEN

In Ecclesiastes 3:1, King Solomon writes: "For everything there is season, a time for every activity under heaven,"(NLV) On Sunday, February 11, 2013, it was indeed the beginning of a new season at Pleasant Green, On this date, the congregation elected Reverend Dr. E. Christopher Jackson as the eleventh pastor of Pleasant Green Missionary Baptist Church.

The election of Reverend Jackson as the eleventh pastor of Pleasant Green would bring many positive changes to the church. First of all, he would be a full-time pastor. Secondly, he was married to Reverend Dr. Coreen Jackson, a beautiful, talented, articulate woman who is also an ordained minister. And finally, he is a father of three talented and energetic teenaged sons, Joshua, Jemiah, and Juleon, who would enhance the membership with their youthful presence and ideas. Pleasant Green would have a new first family. The mood of the congregation was filled with excited anticipation of great things to come. Pastor Jackson suggested that the church should now be referred to as the "Great Pleasant Green". The new church theme would become "Greatness through Godly Growth". It was truly a new season at Pleasant Green. The fellowship period of the morning worship service (passing the peace) was now highlighted by the singing of the song, "A New Season."

> It's a new season; It's is a new day.
> A fresh anointing is flowing my way
> It's a season of power and prosperity too
> It's a new season coming to me.

Shortly after accepting the call to be the next pastor of Pleasant Green, Reverend Jackson met with the congregation on March 18, 2013 to provide information about himself and his Vision and Future Points of Emphasis. The scriptural perspective of this meeting was Proverbs 4:5 *"Get wisdom, get understanding: forget it not, neither decline from the words of my mouth."*

Reverend Jackson began this meeting by sharing information about himself and his leadership style. His leadership style includes the following process: observe, cast vision, train, equip, position and release.

He alluded to the rich history of Pleasant Green and his desire to build on that rich history by helping the church realize its full potential. He suggested that we try to re-build the image of the church in the community into a more positive one. Reverend Jackson then shared his vision of the Core Ministry Values for Pleasant Green. They include:

1) We will be a Loving church
2) We will be a Faith-Walking Church
3) We will be a Praying Church
4) We will be a Word based Church
5) We will be a Christ –Centered Church
6) We will be a Ministry Active Church
7) We will be a Family Oriented Church

Reverend Jackson also shared a list of Transition Team Focus Areas and invited church members to sign up to assist with these teams. The list of teams included:

1) Prayer and Fasting

2) Follow-up of Inactive Pleasant Green members
3) Membership Info Database
4) Photos of Individual Members
5) Church Image and Branding
6) Website Re-vamp
7) Updated Church Bulletin
8) New PG logo and Stationery
9) New Thursday Noon T.N.T. Bible Study (Thursday Noon Togetherr0 11:30-12:30. (Rotating Team Roles: meal, Set-up/Clean-up. Marketing, Hospitality, Materials
10) New member Assimilation Process
11) Fun Committee

Reverend Jackson also discussed Major Capital Renovation Projections, specifically, the implementation of a Faith Lift Fund. The scriptural basis for the creation of this fund is Matthew 7:7 – *"Ask and it shall be given you; seek, and ye shall find; knock and it shall be opened to you."*

Reverend Jackson concluded the meeting by announcing plans for the up-coming Pastoral Installation Weekend. The dates would be Friday, May 31, 2013; Saturday, June 1, and Sunday, June 2, 2013. In preparation for the installation of Reverend Dr. Christopher Jackson as the eleventh pastor of Pleasant Green, an installation steering committee was formed. The members of this committee were Conveners – Deborah Sparks and Julia Moss, Youth Night- DeSean Keys, First Lady's Luncheon- Loyce Thompson, Morning Worship Service- Joel Dobbins and Pierre Moss; Afternoon Worship Service- Walbrey Whitelow and Dr. Samella Spence. Each of these sub-committee chairpersons would come back with progress reports from their committees monthly prior to Installation Weekend.

Youth Night was held Friday, May 31, 2013 at Incredible Dave's in Rivergate Mall. The attendees of this event were the youth of Pleasant Green and the guests of the pastor's three sons: Joshua, Julean, and Jemiah. The youth enjoyed dinner and various video games.

The First Ladies Luncheon was held on Saturday, June1, 2013 at the Baptist World Center Cafeteria. Special tributes to our First Lady, Reverend Dr. Coreen Jackson, were given by Mrs. Mary Lou Davis, the former First Lady of Covenant Baptist Church, Kansas City, Missouri. Mrs. Davis and her husband brought Reverend Coreen from Jamaica during her teenage years and raised and nurtured her through her college years. Additional tributes were given by Mrs. Judith Harrison, and Ms. Sandra Putnam. Special music was rendered by Ms. Demetreus Alexander, and Reverend Willie Thornton, pastor of Mt. Washington Baptist Church, Kansas City, Missouri. The guest speaker was the former First Lady of The Temple Church, Eleanor Graves, and the Mistress of Ceremonies was television personality, Anne Holt from News Channel 2.

The Morning Worship Service featured several musical selections from the guest speaker, Reverend Willie Thornton, pastor of Mt. Washington Missionary Baptist Church, Parkville, Missouri. Reverend Darryl Drumwright, pastor of The Temple Church was the guest speaker at the afternoon Installation service which was held in the auditorium of the Baptist World Center. Congratulatory remarks were given by Reverend Dr. Forrest Harris, Sr., President of American Baptist College. Proclamations were also given to Reverend Jackson from Mayor Karl Dean, Representative Brenda Gilmore, and Senator Thelma Harper. Special music was provided by the combined choirs of the Temple Church and Pleasant Green, and also the Born Again Christian Church Minstrels. The service ended with Fellowship with the First Family in the Baptist World Center Atrium.

After the Pastoral Installation Service, Pastor Jackson began taking the necessary steps to make many of the components of his Pastoral Vision become a reality. On June 30, 2013, Pastor Jackson shared a list of the following accomplishments of his First 100 days as pastor of Pleasant Green:

Physical Plant and Property Improvement
1. Faith Lift Fund: $18,043 +
2. Flat screen monitor for sanctuary
3. Digital clock in sanctuary
4. New church logo, stationery, business cards

5. Church Advertisement investment in <u>Tennessee Tribune</u>
6. Light shade for sanctuary approach area
7. Computer, desk and chair for Receptionist area
8. Paper Folding machine
9. Executive table for lower auditorium
10. Desk, armoire, bookcase, sofa/chair for Pastor's office
11. Pleasant Green Welcome and Core Values banner
12. Installed new floor tiles in lower auditorium
13. Renovated older outside marquee
14. New ceiling tiles on second floor and lower auditorium
15. Three new paper fixtures in restrooms
16. Alignment and securing of wall post
17. Trimmed two large Magnolia trees in front of building
18. Capped off downstairs women's bathroom leaking commode
19. Removed/replaced moldy drywall in women's bathroom
20. Scraped paint from railing on front and side of church, primed railings, wall

Ministry / Programmatic Progress
1. Personal meeting time with the pastor available for each member
2. Member survey
3. New Bulletins
4. Live flowers on sanctuary platform
5. New TNT Bible Study
6. Wednesday Prayer moved to main sanctuary
7. Ministry-focused Pastoral Installation to bond pastor/ people and elevate church image
8. One returned member and one Candidate for Baptism
9. Visitation of Sick & Shut-in
10. Wednesday Bible Study walk Through
11. Practical, Demonstrative sermons and 8-part Core Values Series
12. Membership and participation in the Interdenominational Ministerial Fellowship
13. Establishing rapport with area businesses
14. Participation of family members in life of congregation
15. Renewal of Strategic Partnership with Grace Park Church
16. Electronic Communication between pulpit and AV station
17. Planning with Vacation Bible School Committee
18. Meetings with Deacons, Trustees, Vacations Bible School Group

2014 Projection Developments:
1. Spruce Up Day- Saturday. June 27th'- laptop computer; lower auditorium AC repair
2. Siding on front windows and wood replacement on top molding
3. Roof Repair (flashing, patching, tarp covering)
4. Renovation of sanctuary, rear entryway, lower auditorium, front yard landscaping
5. Third floor renovation (AC unit, floors, bathroom, etc.)
6. New PG Web Site
7. Outreach to Fisk, Meharry, Tennessee State University
8. Outreach to Business Community
9. Regular Advertising in Tennessee Tribune, and 92Q radio station
10. Pleasant Green Leadership Retreat
11. Quarterly Congregational Fun Activity
12. Membership and participation in J.U.M.P.

13. Digital Signage in Front of Church
14. Carpet Cleaning or Replacement
15. Youth, Young Adult, College Ministry Development
16. Marriage and Relationship Ministry
17. Participation of guest Artistic groups and individuals

Pastoral Commitments and Congregational Expectations:

1. Pastoral Attitude and Atmosphere of Excellence, Openness, and Accountability
2. Quarterly Trustee Financial Report and attitude of excellence and openness
3. Culture of bombarding all PG visitors with sincere love, welcome and follow-up
4. Leader and Congregational Involvement in personal/corporate Bible Study and tithing
5. Pleasant attitude and atmosphere of love and cooperation with everyone
6. Regular habit of praying for, verbally promoting and inviting others to PG (1 Corinthians: 6-7)
7. Music and worship that is excellent, balanced and Christ-centered
8. Incorporate the eight Core values as we pursue Greatness through Godly Growth.

The members of Pleasant Green were truly encouraged by this list of accomplishments in such a short period of time and truly anticipated that better times were on the horizon for Pleasant Green.

Pictorial Highlights

of the

FIRST LADY'S LUNCHEON

Honoring

REVEREND DR. COREEN DAWKINS JACKSON

SATURDAY, JUNE 1, 2013
BAPTIST WORLD CENTER
NASHVILLE, TENNESSEE 37204

The First Lady's Luncheon

of the

PLEASANT GREEN MISSIONARY BAPTIST CHURCH

Honoring

REVEREND DR. COREEN DAWKINS JACKSON

SATURDAY, JUNE 1, 2013

WORLD BAPTIST CENTER CAFETERIA

11:30 A.M.

First Lady's Luncheon

Honoring
Reverend Dr. Coreen Jackson

Baptist World Center 1700 Baptist World Center Drive
Nashville, TN 37207

Mrs. Anne Holt, Mistress of Ceremonies

The Music	Selected Recordings
The Welcome and Introduction of MC	Mrs. Loyce Thompson Luncheon Chair
The Scripture	Mrs. Kimberly Cannon
The Invocation/Blessing of Food	Minister Benita McLean

LUNCH IS SERVED
(Video presentation of the Life of Reverend Dr. Coreen Jackson)

The Music	Ms. Demetrus Alexander
The Reflections	Mrs. Mary Lou Davis Former First Lady, Covenant Baptist Church Kansas City, Missouri
The Reflections	Mrs. Judith Harrison
The Reflections	Reverend Patricia Brock Associate Minister, The Temple Church
The Introduction of Speaker	Mrs. LaTosha Warfield
The Music	Reverend Willie Thornton Pastor, Mt. Washington Baptist Church Kansas City, Missouri
The Speaker	Mrs. Eleanor Graves Former First lady, The Temple Church
The Prayer for the First Lady	Pastor Cynthia Macon Gordon The Temple Church
Special Presentation (to the First Lady)	Deacon Roxie Johnson
The First Lady Speaks	Reverend Dr. Coreen Jackson
The Door Prizes	Ms. Jennifer Johnson
The Remarks	Reverend E. Christopher Jackson Pastor, Pleasant Green Baptist Church
The Benediction	Reverend E. Christopher Jackson

THE FIRST LADY'S LUNCHEON COMMITTEE

HONOREE: REV. DR. COREEN JACKSON ESCORTED BY REV. DR. CHRISTOPHER JACKSON

MRS. LOYCE THOMPSON, LUNCHEON CHAIRPERSON

MRS. MARY LOU DAVIS, MRS. JUDITH HARRISON
MRS. ANNIE HOLT

MRS. ELEANOR GRAVES, MINISTER BENITA MCLEAN
KIM CAMPBELL, LATOSHA WARFIELD

MRS. ELEANOR GRAVES, GUEST SPEAKER

REVEREND WILLIE THORNTON

MRS. ELIZABETH HESTER, DR. HENRIETTA MCCALLISTER
MRS. WANDA SCOTT

REVEREND DR. COREEN JACKSON, HONOREE

CAITLYN GILLESPIE, BRIANA GILLESPIE
MRS. RUBY BURFORD

MRS. VIRGINIA BROOKS, MS. BEVERLY BARTON
MS. MADELINE BARTON

MS. LIFRAN FORT, MRS. CARMELIA TATE
MS. NYENA GREER

MS. ERIKA MARTIN, MRS. BETTY BARNETT
DEACON HARRY BARNETT

MRS. ROXIE JOHNSON
MRS. DEMETRIUS ALEXANDER

ARTHUR THOMPSON
ANNIE HOLT
LOUIS KING
LOYCE THOMPSON

REV. DR. CHRISTOPHER JACKSON
HONOREE, REV. COREEN JACKSON

The Installation-Investiture Services

Eleventh Pastor

PLEASANT GREEN MISSIONARY BAPTIST CHURCH

REVEREND E. CHRISTOPHER JACKSON, D. MIN.

· · · · · · · ·

SUNDAY, JUNE 2, 2013

3:00 P.M.

BAPTIST WORLD CENTER

NASHVILLE, TENNESSEE 37204

Dedication to

Mrs. Christine Jackson

June 7, 1918–July 8, 2011

In Precious Memory and Loving Dedication to the Memory of the Pastor's Mother,
we dedicate these Installation-Investiture Services of the eleventh Pastor
of Pleasant Green Missionary Baptist Church
Reverend Dr. E. Christopher Jackson

*precious memories, unseen angels, sent from somewhere to my soul;
How they linger, even new me, and the sacred past unfold….
As I travel on life's pathway, know not what the years may hold;
As I ponder, hope grows fonder,
Precious memories flood my soul"

Combs/Wright

The Mirror

Sunday, June 2, 2013   **Communion Sunday**   **10:00 A.M.**

The Order of Worship

*The Call to Worship .... Reverend Pierre Moss

*The Invocation... Reverend Pierre Moss

The Worship Praise Music.. Mr. Jesse White, the Temple Church

The Welcome/June Birthdays...Pastor E. Christopher Jackson

"It's A New Season"

The Music...Reverend W. Thornton, Pastor

    ("Praise is What I Do")..................................... Mt. Washington Baptist Church, Kansas City, Missouri

The Observations ....Deacon Richard Friley

The Children's Message... Mrs. Brandy Thornton, Kansas City

The Ministry of Tithing and Giving .... Deacon Henry Stinson

Music:...'Walk With Me"-Men's Ensemble .... Prayer *Doxology

The Scripture .... Reverend Pierre Moss

The Introduction of Guest Speaker...Pastor E. Chris Jackson

The Preparation Music ....Worship Chorale

The Sermon..Reverend Willie M. Thornton

The Invitation to Disciple ....Pastor E. Christopher Jackson

The Invitation Music.. Choir and Congregation

The Words of Encouragement...Mrs. Brandy Thornton
                                                                                                                                        Reverend Willie Thornton

The Altar Call, Prayer .... Reverend Pierre Moss

The Lord's Supper

The Scripture: 1st Corinthians 11:23-29 .... Deacon Bernard Sparks

The Prayer-----The Distribution of the Bread and Wine--------The Music

*The Benediction ....Pastor E. Christopher Jackson

The Installation-Investiture Service
of the Eleventh Pastor of
Pleasant Green Missionary Baptist Church
Reverend E. Christopher Jackson, D. Min.

Sunday, June 2, 2013 Baptist World Center 3:00 P.M.

The Service Prelude: Praise and Worship	Mass Choir
	Jesse White, The Temple Church
The Seating of the First Family	The Marshalls
The Processional	The Dais
*The Hymn	Choir and Congregation

"Great is Thy Faithfulness"

1. "Great is Thy faithfulness" O 'God, my Father, there is no shadow of turning With Thee,. Thou changest not, Thy compassions, they fail not, As Thou hast Been Thou forever will be.

Refrain

"Great is Thy faithfulness! Great is Thy faithfulness!" Morning by morning new Mercies I see; all I have needed Thy hand hath provided. "Great is Thy faithfulness," Lord unto me!

2. Summer and winter, and springtime and harvest, sun, moon and stars iin their Courses above, join with all nature in manifold witness to Thy great faithfulness, Mercy and love.

3. Pardon for sin and a peace that endureth, thine own dear presence to cheer and To guide; Strength for today and bright hope for tomorrow, blessings all mine, with ten thousands beside!

The Call to Worship/Occasion	Reverend Dr./ Judy Cummings, Pastor
	New Covenant Christian Church, Disciples of Christ
The Invocation	Reverend Bob Cook, Pastor
	The Church of Grace Park, White House, TN
The Music	Born Again Christian Church Minstrels
The Scriptures: The Old Testament-Isaiah 40:28-31	Reverend Ron Trail, The Temple Church
The New Testament-John 15:5-8	Reverend Dr. Evelyn Barbour, Pleasant Green
The Music	Mass Choirs
The Welcome	Deacon Walbrey Whitelow
	Sunday afternoon Installation Chairperson, Pleasant Green Church
The Presentation	State of Tennessee Representative Brenda Gilmore
The Recognition of Guests	Reverend Judy Cummings
The Pastoral Greeting	Reverend James Thomas, Pastor
	Jefferson Street Baptist Church

The Ministry of Giving	Reverend James Thomas
The Offertory Prayer	Reverend Inman Otey, Pastor
	Zion New Jerusalem Baptist Church
The Introduction of the Speaker	Reverend Victor Wynn, Minister of Worship
	Assistant Pastor, The Temple Church
The Music	Mass Choirs
The Sermon	Reverend Darrell Drumwright, Pastor
	The Temple Church
The Invitation to Discipleship	Reverend Pierre Moss, Assistant Pastor, Pleasant Green Baptist Church
The Recognition: Search Committee	Reverend Dr. Samella W. Junior Spence
	Staff Administrator, Minister of Music, Pleasant Green Church
The Charge to Pastor and First Lady	Bishop Horace and Elder Kiwanis Hockett
	Pastor and First Lady, Born Again Christian Church
The Covenant Charge of Pastor and People	Reverend Curtis Bender
	The Temple Church

Leader: In the name of the Lord Jesus Christ, the Kind and Head of the Church, and in His Presence, we are met as a congregation to install as minister of historic Pleasant Green Missionary Baptist Church, the Reverend Dr. E. Christopher Jackson. Inasmuch as this solemn act involves mutual obligation, I will call upon you to unite in a covenant of dedication. Let the minister to be installed stand and make his declaration.

Minister: Willingly do I affirm my ordination vow: Believing with all my heart that Jesus is the Christ, the Son of the Living God, and accepting the Holy Scriptures Inspired of God through the Holy Spirit, it is my sincere desire to devote my Life to the ministry of the Word, so to live as to bring credit to the gospel Which I preach and to fulfill to my utmost ability the office of a good minister Of Jesus Christ.

Leader: Will the ministers, officers and members of Pleasant Green Missionary Baptist Church stand and make your declaration? (Pleasant Green members stand) Do you affirm y9ur membership in Christ's church, and your fellowship in the Congregation with those who have obtained a like precious faith, renewing your Vows of fidelity to our Lord Jesus Christ, and your allegiance to His church? Do You solemnly covenant to work together with your minister to extend the gospel In its purity and power in the community and throughout the world and, as faithful Servants of the Lord, to give your pastor your utmost support in every way, According to your abilities and opportunities?

Congregation: We do.

Minister: Brothers and Sisters, standing with you, I affirm my willingness to be your minister And now convene with you that in the s trength and grace of our Lord Jesus Christ, I will live a holy and circumspect life among you, for an example, and will dillgently And faithfully endeavor to perform all the duties of a good minister of Jesus Christ On behalf of this congregation to the glory of His Name the edification of His church.

Leader: In the Name of our Lord Jesus Christ, the King and Head of the Church, we do hereby declare you, Reverend Dr. E. Christopher Jackson to be properly installed as the Minister of the gospel and Pastor of t his congregation, In token thereof, I give you the Right hand of fellowship. The grace of our Lord Jesus Christ be with you. Amen

The Installation Prayer .... Elder Barry Towles, Born Again Christian Church

The Investiture of the Pastor

       The Robe .... De'Sean Keys, Young Adult, Pleasant Green Baptist Church
                                                          Pastor's Sons: Joshua, Juleon and Jemiah Jackson

       The Bible .... Deacon Bernard Sparks, Diaconal Chairman, Pastor's Father: Andrew Jackson, Sr.

       The Hymn book .... Reverend Willie A. Thornton, Elijah Daniels, Children's Ministry
                                                                Pastor's Spouse, Reverend Coreen Jackson

       The Keys .... Trustee Henrietta McCallister, and son, Former Trustee Michaelangelo McCallister

The Gathering of all Ministers for the Laying on of Hands and Prayer

The Response/Remarks .... Reverend E. Christian Jackson, D.Min., Pastor
                                                                               The Great Pleasant Green Missionary Baptist Church

The Choral Benediction .... Mass Choirs

The Recessional .... Pastor/First Lady/Family/Dais

The Fellowship with the First Family follows in the Baptist World Center Atrium

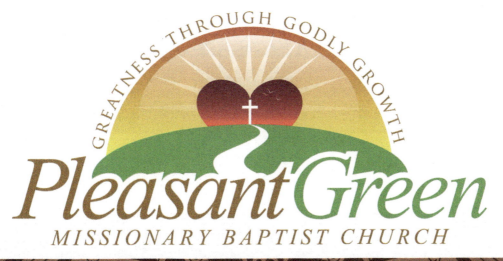

Pictorial Highlights

of the

INSTALLATION- INVESTITURE SERVICES

For

REVEREND DR. E. CHRISTOPHER JACKSON, D. MIN.

ELEVENTH PASTOR

PLEASANT GREEN MISSIONARY BAPTIST CHURCH

SUNDAY, JUNE 2, 2013
BAPTIST WORLD CENTER
NASHVILLE, TENNESSEE 37204

Reverend Dr. Christopher Jackson

Reverend Darrell A. Drumwright, Pastor the Temple Church

Reverend Dr. Forrest E. Harris, Sr., President, American Baptist College
American Baptist Church

Bishop Horace and Elder Kiwanis Hockett
Pastor and First Lady of Born Again Christian Church

Born Again Christian Church Minstrels

Ms. Kimberly Fleming

Presentation of the Bible to Pastor Jackson
Deacon Bernard Sparks and Andrew Jackson, Sr., Pastor's Father

Pastor Jackson and Family
Sons: Juleon, Joshua, Jemiah, and First Lady Reverend Dr. Coreen Jackson

Church Covenant:

Having been led, as we believe, by the Holy Spirit of God to receive the Lord Jesus Christ as Saviour, and on the profession of our faith, having been Baptized in the name of the Father, and of the Son, and of the Holy Ghost, we do now in the presence of God, angels, and this assembly most solemnly and joyfully enter into covenant with one another, as one body in Christ.

We engage, therefore by the aid of the Holy Spirit, to walk together in Christian love; to strive for the advancement of this Church in knowledge, holiness, and comfort; to promote its prosperity and spirituality; to sustain its worship, ordinances, discipline, and doctrine; to contribute cheerfully and regularly to the ministry, to the expenses of the church, the relief of the poor, and the spread of the Gospel through all nations.

We also engage to maintain family and secret devotion; to educate our children consistently; to seek the salvation of our kindred and acquaintances; to walk circumspectly in the world; to be just in our dealings, faithful in our engagements, and exemplary in our deportment; to avoid all tattling, backbiting, and excessive anger to abstain from the use of intoxicating drink and illegal drugs, and to be zealous in our efforts to advance the Kingdom of our Saviour

We further engage to watch over one another in brotherly love: to remember each other in prayer; to aid each other in sickness and distress; to cultivate Christian sympathy in feeling and courtesy in speech; to be slow to take offense, but always ready for reconciliation, and mindful of the rules of our Saviour to secure it without delay.

We moreover engage that, when we remove from this place, we will as soon as possible unite with some other church where we can carry out the spirit of this covenant and the principles of God's Word

Church Organizational Pictures
The Ministerial Staff

Rev. Pierre Moss, Rev. dr. Samella Spence, Rev. Dr. Christopher Jackson, Senior Pastor
Rev. Dr. Coreen Jackson, Rev. Dr. Evelyn Barbour

The Deacon's Ministry

1st Row: William Johnson, Henry Stinson
2nd Row: Roxie Johnson, Cordelia Wakefield
3rd Row: Harry Barnett, Walbrey Whitelow, Julius Hill
4th Row: Hanry Berry, Charles Gillespie, Bernard Sparks, Chairman
Not Shown: Richard Friley, Victoria Lewis

The Trustee's Ministry

1st Row: Isaac Buford, Preston Mitchell
2nd Row: Jennifer Johnson, Julia Moss, Kimberly Cannon, Madeline Barton
Not Shown: Angela Dobbins, Joel Dobbins, Latosha Warfield, Louis King

The Usher's Ministry

1st Row: Anita Hill, President, Shirlyn Johnson, Wanda Hill, Carmelia Tate
2nd Row: Judy Sanders, Tim Warfield, Letitia Howell

The Ladies Aid Society

Seated: Mary Hamby, Hattie McKay, Walbrey Whitelow, President, Rebecca Jennings
Bernardeen Fleming, Samella Spence
2nd Row: Karen Johnson, Helena Merritt, Vivian Berry, Coreen Jackson, Franchetta Greer
Connie Carter, Loyce Thompson, Carmelia Tate
3rd Row: Ruby Burford, Evelyn Barbour, Theodora Howell, Gloria Lewis,
Lifran Fort, Letitia Howell, Tallujah Shinault
Not Shown: Eunice Grisby, Sarah Wilhoite, Henrietta McCallister, Lenay Ruffin
Florence Anderson

The Men's Ministry

Seated: William Johnson, Henry Stinson
1st Row: Harry Barnett, Louis King, President
2nd Row: Herman Brady, Herman Dixon, Preston Mitchell, Clarence Goldsten
3rd Row: Isaac Burford, Henry Berry, Charles Gillespie, Bernard Sparks, Theodore Lewis

The Children's Choir

1st Row: Taivon Moore, Xavier Moss, Gionni Moss, Isaiah Moss, Daijon Berry
2nd Row: Madeline Barton, Director, Karbyn Cannon, LePrecious Wilkerson, Nyena Foxworth, Alijah Daniels Beverly Barton Director

The Adult Choir

1st Row: Jennifer Johnson, Angela Dobbins, Kimberly Cannon, Latosha Warfield, Candace Moss, Marilyn Hiner, Doris Dobbins, Tyesha Jackson, Erica Martin, Roxie Johnson, Caitlyn Gillespie, Nita Smith, Director
2nd Row: Tyronne Hamilton, Tim Hamilton, Xavier Moss, Joel Dobbins, C. C. Johnson

The College Ministry

1st Row: Jennifer Johnson, Kristen Brown
2nd Row: Kimberly Cannon, Rev. Pierre Moss, Candace Moss

Reverend Christopher Jackson, Reverend Coreen Jackson, Reverend Pierre Moss

THE ROOM-IN-THE INN'S MINISTRY

1st Row: Julius Hill
Herman Brady, Judy Sanders
Herman Dixon
2nd Clarence Goldsten
Wanda Hill, Chairman
Bernard Sparks
3rd Row: Madeline Barton
Harry Barnett, Betty Barnett
Deborah Sparks, Beverly Barton

Not Shown: Richard Friley, Sharon Friley, Belinda Lee, Wilson Lee

THE HISTORY COMMITTEE

1st Row: Beverly Barton
Wanda Scott,
Loyce Thompson, Chair
Walbrey Whitelow
2nd Row: Madeline Barton
Theodora Howell,
Henry Berry, Ruby Burford
Lifran Fort

Not Shown: Doris Dobbins

Sunday School Class

Seated: Henry Stinson
Standing: Rev. Evelyn Barbour, Mary Beene, Cordelia Wakefield, Candace Moss, Jennifer Johnson, Kristen Brown

Deborah Sparks
Church Clerk

Momentous Events
2003-2013
at
PLEASANT GREEN MISSIONARY BAPTIST CHURCH

Pleasant Green Missionary Baptist Church
1410 Jefferson Street
Nashville, Tennessee
Reverend Dr. Alvin E. Miller, Sr., Pastor

Laymen's League
Weekend of Spiritual Uplift

Friday, May 27, 2005   7:00 P.M.
    Reverend Breonus Mitchell, Preacher
    Greater Grace Temple Church Choir

Saturday, May 28. 2005   9:00 A. M.
    Prayer Breakfast
    Reverend William Harris, Preacher
    Galilee Baptist Church

Music: Men of Thunder

*****

Sunday, May 29, 2005

9:00 A.M. Sunday School   10:45 A.M. Worship
    Reverend Dr. Alvin E. Miller, Sr., Preacher
    Music: Pleasant Green Men's Chorus

Sunday, May 29, 2005   Musical Gala   4:00 P. M.
    Damon King, Master of Ceremonies
    Lee Chapel AME Men's Chorus
    Olivet Baptist Church Men's Chorus
    Cleveland Street Baptist Church Men's Chorus
    Kayne Avenue Baptist Church Men's Chorus
    Westwood Baptist Church Men's Chorus
    Mount Calvary Baptist Church Men's Chorus (Madison, TN)
    Jefferson Street Baptist Church Men's Chorus

Pleasant Green Missionary Baptist Church

presents

a

Fine Arts Celebration

Art
Wood Sculpture
Music
Dance
Drama
Poetry

and

Guest Artist

Reverend Dr. Sherman Roosevelt Tribble

Sunday, October 29, 2006　　　　　　　　3:00 P.M.
Pleasant Green Missionary Baptist Church
1410 Jefferson Street
Nashville, Tennessee
Reverend Dr. Alvin E. Miller, Sr., Pastor

The Fine Arts Ministry
Pleasant Green Missionary Baptist Church

presents

Herman D. Brady

(Retired Professor- Tennessee State University)

in

GOD'S Trombones

(James Weldon Johnson)
and
The Church Sanctuary Choir - Spirituals

Sunday, September 30, 2007
4:00 P.M.

Pleasant Green Missionary Baptist Church
1410 Jefferson Street
Nashville, TN 37208
Reverend Dr. Alvin E. Miller, Sr., Pastor

Pleasant Green Missionary Baptist Church

Laymen's League Weekend Celebration
Theme: "Christian Men Ministering in God's Vineyard

Prayer Breakfast	Morning Worship Service	Afternoon Service
Saturday, July 21, 2007	Sunday, July 22, 2007	Sunday, July 22, 2007
Speaker	Speaker	Speaker
Rev. James Thomas	Rev. Dr. Alvin Miller, Sr.	Rev. Darrell Drumwright
Jefferson Street Baptist Church	Pleasant Green Baptist Church	The Temple Church
Music: Jefferson Street Men's Chorus	Pleasant Green Men's Chorus	The Temple Men's Chorus

Pleasant Green Missionary Baptist Church

1410 Jefferson Street
Nashville, Tennessee 37208

Reverend Dr. Alvin E. Miller, Sr., Pastor

"The Best is Yet to Come" (Haggai 2:9)

OMEGA PSI PHI FRATERNITY, INC.

4TH ANNUAL "QUES FOR CHRIST" REVIVAL

OMEGA LAMBDA LAMBDA CHAPTER

Monday August 4, 2008
Presiding Elder Ralph E. Johnson
Tuesday August 5, 2008
Rev. Elmore Torbert, Jr.
Wednesday August 6, 2008
Rev. Harold M. Love, Jr.
Thursday August 7, 2008
Rev. Jerry Maynard, II
Friday August 8, 2008
Rev. L. Rodney Bennett

Pleasant Green Missionary Baptist Church

1410 Jefferson Street

Nashville, TN 37208

August 4–8, 2008

6:00 PM

The Ladies' Aid Society
of
Pleasant Green Missionary Baptist Church
Celebrates its 60th Anniversary
in a

Musical Salute

to

Fisk University
Fisk Jubilee Singers

Special Guests
Former Fisk Jubilee Singers
Dr. Matthew Kennedy
Former Director, Fisk Jubilee Singers

Sunday, May 20, 2012
3:00 P.M.

Pleasant Green Missionary Baptist Church
1410 Jefferson Street
Nashville, Tennessee 37208

Mrs. Mary L. Hamby, President
Reverend Pierre Moss, Assistant Pastor

Pulpit, Pew & Public

Pleasant Green Ladies Aid Society honors Fisk Univ

1st row: Mrs. Hattie McKay, and Rev. James Sawyers
2nd row: First Baptist, Capital Hill Choir

Mt. Nebo Church Choir

The Ladies Aid Society of Pleasant Green Baptist Church recently celebrated its anniversary with a 'Musical Salute to Fisk University and the Fisk Jubilee Singers.' Special guests for the event included: Dr. Matthew Kennedy, former director of the Jubilee Singers; and five former Fisk Jubilee singers, including Ms. Kimberly Fleming, Ms. Debra Tillery, Ms. Jackie Hannah, and Mr. Erskine Lytle. A fifth former Jubilee singer, Rev. James Sawyers, delivered a sermonic meditation.

The Ladies Aid Society wanted to make this years' anniversary celebration a community celebration, so the choirs of First Baptist Church, Capital Hill, and Mt. Nebo Baptist Church, and the Blue Notes of Zeta Phi Beta Sorority were also invited as special guests.

The musical selections included old favorites like 'Jesus is the Light,' 'My Soul Has Been Anchored in the Lord,' 'Total Praise,' and 'My Tribute.'

Rev. Dr. Edith Kimbrough and Dr. Matthew Kennedy

The musical highlight of the evening occurred when Dr. Matthew Kennedy, the honoree, played a medley of religious songs at the piano. At 95, Dr. Kennedy demonstrated that he still possesses the extraordinary musical talent that has helped him to achieve local, national, and international fame as a concert pianist.

At the conclusion of his musical selections, he was presented with tokens of appreciation from Rev. Dr. Edith Kimbrough.

The Ladies Aid Society of Pleasant Green Baptist Church was organized over half a century ago. Over the years, the Ladies Aid Society has evidenced their presence in the community by giving aid to individuals, organizations, and institutions where needed.

They have assisted victims of natural disasters in Haiti, Florida, Louisiana, and most recently the victims of the Nashville Flood of 2010. The goal of the anniversary musical was to raise money for Fisk

Mrs. Mary L Hamby,
President
Ladies Aid Society

University. The Ladies Aid Society was pleased to donate $1500 to Fisk from the proceeds of the program.

The president of the Ladies Aid Society, Mrs. Mary L. Hamby, said she was grateful to the church, community, and all the participants who gave of their time and money in support of this fundraiser for Fisk. Without this kind of support, the gift would not have been possible.

Fall Revival 2012
Of
Pleasant Green Missionary Baptist Church
1410 Jefferson Street Nashville, TN. 37208

Monday-Wednesday: November 26-28, 2012
6:30 pm – 8:30 pm
Theme: *"Spiritual Renewal Through Transition"*

Sponsor:
The Ladies' Aid Society
Pleasant Green Baptist Church

Guest Evangelist:

Reverend John R. Faison, Sr., Pastor
Watson Grove Missionary Baptist Church
Nashville, Tennessee

Meeting of the Ladies Aid Society
Pleasant Green Baptist Church
Sunday, December 16, 2012

AGENDA

Call to Order – Deacon Walbrey R. Whitelow, President
The Monthly Theme– Scripture -Grace – Mrs. Sarah H. Wilhoite, Chaplain
Refreshments.........December Hostesses
Mrs. Vivian Berry, Mrs. Hattie L. McKay, Ms. Franchetta Greer

. . . .

Thank You
DR. SAMELLA JUNIOR SPENCE

The Ladies Aid Society and Pleasant Green Baptist Church Appreciate You!

Expressions of Appreciation (Limit 2 minutes please)
Dr. Edith W. Kimbrough
Mrs. Ruby Burford
Sister Rebecca Jennings
Deacon Bernard Sparks
Trustee Kim Cannon
Rev. Pierre Moss

A Special Reflection . . . .   Mrs. Gloria Lewis

Presentations . . Mrs. Mary L. Hamby, Immediate Past President
Ms. Shanel Thompson and Ms. Leticia Howell

Response . . . . Dr. Samella Junior Spence

Benediction . . . . Dr. Edith W. Kimbrough, Past President

. . . .

The Ladies Aid Society
Wishes Each of You and Your Families a Very Merry Christmas!

Dr. Samella Spence, Honoree

Pictorial Highlights

of

The Sixty-first Anniversary Celebration

of the

Ladies Aid Society

Sunday, June 23, 2013

The Honorees

Dr. Eunice Grisby escorted by Deacon Bernard Sparks

Mrs. Mary Hamby escorted by Trustee Louis King

Mrs. Rebecca Jennings escorted by Deacon Henry Berry

Dr. Henrietta McCallister escorted by Deacon Charles Gillespie

Mrs. Hattie McKay escorted by Deacon Harry Barnett

Mrs. Sarah Wilhoite escorted by Trustee Emeritus Theodore Lewis

About the Honorees

Dr. Eunice Grisby –
Over the years Dr. Grisby has given extensive service to her church and the community. At Pleasant Green her leadership roles have included being Sunday School Superintendent, Chairman of the Building Committee for the Andrew l. Porter Educational Annex, President of the Ladies Aid Society and providing leadership in an Adult Literacy Program in connection with the Metropolitan Public School System.

Mrs. Mary Lean Hamby
Mrs. Hamby joined pleasant Green in 1942. As the daughter of a minister, attending church and rendering service to the church have always been prominent goals for Sister Hamby . During her 72 years of membership at pleasant Green, Mrs. Hamby has served as President of the Ladies Aid Society twice. She has also provided leadership in the Annual Prayer Breakfast, and community service projects for Haiti, Katrina victims, and goody bags for area college students.

Mrs. Rebecca Jennings
As the daughter of an Elder in the church, and the wife of a minister, Mrs. Jennings came from a spiritual family where service in the church was a high priority. Mrs. Jennings joined Pleasant Green after her service in World War II as a medical technician. During her 76 years of membership at Pleasant Green, she has provided leadership in her role as President of the Ladies Aid Society, head of the Baptist Training Union (BTU), and as a teacher in the Sunday School. Mrs. Jennings wish is to see her church thrive and stand for years to come.

Dr. Henrietta McCallister
Dr. McCallister has had a life- long commitment to education as revealed in her many years of service as a Principal in the Metropolitan Nashville Public School system, Associate Professor of Psychology at Tennessee State University, and as a Ford Foundation Coordinator of the Reading Clinic. She has cherished her membership in the Ladies Aid calling it one of her "most rewarding experiences". She appreciates the loving and helpful attitude that the Ladies Aid Society extends to everyone in need. She prays that the members' love for each other will continue to grow, being led by the theme of the of the organization—"Women Mentoring Women through Love".

Mrs. Hattie McKay
Mrs. McKay joined Pleasant Green in 1969 under the pastorate of Reverend Andrew l. Porter, Jr., now deceased. She has been active throughout her years of membership at Pleasant Green serving in several ministries. She has especially enjoyed her membership in the Ladies Aid Society because of its focus on Christian women who are studying the Word of God, and following the teachings of Jesus Christ as they provide aid to others. Through her employment as a librarian in the Marietta, Georgia and Metropolitan Nashville School system, she has attempted to extend her Christian experiences through serving others.

Mrs. Sarah Wilhoite
Mrs. Wilhoite joined Pleasant Green in August of 1942, and was baptized under the pastorate of Reverend I.H. Henderson. She has been active throughout her years at Pleasant Green serving in several ministry areas, but mainly in the Music Ministry as a frequently requested soloist. Teaching was her profession and she first taught Home Economics in Dickson, Tennessee followed by teaching first, second and third grades in the Metropolitan Public School System. Mrs. Wilhoite currently serves as Chaplain of the Ladies Aid Society.

Pleasant Green Ladies Aid Society celebrates anniversary

1st row: left to right- Eunice Grisby, Mary Hamby, Walbrey Whitelow, Hattie McKay, Rebecca Jennings, and Sarah Wilhoite 2nd row left to right- Ruby Burford, Theodora Howell, Edith kimbrough, Vivian Berry, Franchetta Greer, Loyce Thompson, Deborah Sparks, Florence Anderson, Latitia Howell. Not pictured Henrietta McCallister

by Wanda Clay

On June 24th The Ladies Aid Society of Pleasant Green Missionary Baptist Church will gather to celebrate its 61st anniversary. The service will be held at 3:00 pm at Pleasant Green, 1410 Jefferson Street. The theme for the occasion is "Celebrating the Legacy." This celebration will honor six members of the Ladies Aid Society who has given over 50 years of service to the church and to the community.

The Ladies Aid Society is an organization that fulfills a diverse range of duties and responsibilities. Members siad, "As the name suggests, they have been ready to assist whenever and however needed." The society has assisted victims of natural disasters in Haiti., Florida, and Louisiana, and the Nashville flood of 2010. The organization has also conducted Adult Literacy programs, and donated electronics and appliances to persons in need of assistance.

The honorees are: Dr. Eunice Campbell Grisby, Mrs. Mary Hamby, Mrs. Rebecca Jennings, Dr. Henrietta McCallister, Mrs. Hattie McKay, and Mrs. Sarah Wilhoite. "All six honorees have served in various leadership positions in the church, and all six are retired Metro schools teachers and administrators," stated program organizers.

The celebration will consist of special music provided by Mrs. Audrey Bowie, recording artist, former Minister of Music at Spruce Street Baptist Church, and former choral music instructor at Stratford High School.

The speaker for this anniversary service will be Reverend Dr. Coreen Jackson, Professor of Communication, and now the new Director of the Honors Center at Tennessee State University. She is the mother of three teenage sons, and is married to Rev. Dr. E. Christopher Jackson, the newly installed pastor of Pleasant Green Baptist Church.

For further information, contact the church office @ (615) 329-1189.

CPSIA information can be obtained at www.ICGtesting.com
Printed in the USA
LVOW05*1118050415

433151LV00002BA/3/P